101
Favorite
Saltwater Flies

101
Favorite
Saltwater Flies

HISTORY, TYING TIPS, AND FISHING STRATEGIES

by
David Klausmeyer

Skyhorse Publishing

Skyhorse Publishing books may be purchased in bulk at special discounts for sales promotion, corporate gifts, fund-raising, or educational purposes. Special editions can also be created to specifications. For details, contact the Special Sales Department, Skyhorse Publishing, 307 West 36th Street, 11th Floor, New York, NY 10018 or info@skyhorsepublishing.com.

Skyhorse® and Skyhorse Publishing® are registered trademarks of Skyhorse Publishing, Inc.®, a Delaware corporation.

Visit our website at www.skyhorsepublishing.com.

10 9 8 7 6 5 4 3 2 1

Library of Congress Cataloging-in-Publication Data is available on file.

Cover design by Owen Corrigan

ISBN: 978-1-63220-538-4
Ebook ISBN: 978-1-63220-951-1

Printed in China

Contents

Chapter 3
Flats Flies: Patterns for Fishing Skinny Water   125

Introduction

WHAT TYPE OF FISH DO YOU WANT TO CATCH: STRIPED BASS, bluefish, false albacore, bonefish, permit, snook, or tarpon? Perhaps you have another species of fish in mind: redfish, bonito, barracuda, snapper, or something else. Our oceans are chock-full of worthy targets, but you will need the right flies to attract them.

101 Favorite Saltwater Flies is a smorgasbord of great patterns designed to catch a wide variety of our favorite gamefish. In addition to the fly recipes, I include histories and offer insights about how to fish or tie them. The stories of these flies are as varied as the patterns themselves. Eat as much as you like, and then come back for more.

A great many anglers have played key roles in my development as a fly fisherman and tier. Without them, my life and fishing would be poorer. The following folks—in no particular order—have offered important contributions to this book, and I offer them my thanks. Tie or buy their flies, and you will catch fish.

Dick Brown
Al Ritt
Drew Chicone
Bob Veverka
Aaron Adams
Tim Borski
Alan Caolo
Lefty Kreh
Patrick Dorsey
Tom McQuade
Bob Clouser
Dan Blanton
Bob Popovics
Lou Tabory
Craig Mathews
Matt Ramsey

Kirk Dietrich

Brad Buzzi

Stu Apte

Joe Blados

Jack Gartside

Mike Hogue

Barry and Cathy Beck

John Kumiski.

Henry Cowen

Lenny Moffo

Chris Newsome

Peter Smith

Jonny King

Steve Farrar

Thomas Kintz

Page Rogers

Kate and Bill Howe

David Skok

Keith Fulsher

Bob Hines

Chuck Furimsky

Art Sheck

Richard Murphy

Lex Hochner

Greg Miheve

CHAPTER ONE

Attractor Patterns:
Flies for Fishing
Anytime and Anywhere

Black Death

Hook: Tiemco TMC600 SP, sizes 2 to 4/0.
Thread: Red 3/0.
Tail: Black saddle hackles.
Collar: Gray squirrel tail hair dyed red.
Nose: Red tying thread.

THERE ARE A LOT OF TARPON PATTERNS CALLED BLACK
Death. When writing this book, it was tough to choose which Black Death
to include. Maybe, because there are several versions of this pattern, it really
doesn't matter: when getting ready for your next tarpon-fishing adventure,
just be sure to include a selection of dark-colored flies.

Hook selection is critical. Hooks for tarpon flies are made using heavy
wire. These hooks are extremely strong to catch these fierce-fighting fish. A
tarpon's mouth is also very hard, so these hooks are extremely sharp—sharper
than many other hooks—so they sink home. The shanks are usually slightly
short and the points are curved up, which also helps in hooking tarpon.

The pattern recipe recommends the Tiemco TMC600 SP for tying the
Black Death. This hook is widely available, but you may substitute with any
similar hook. Tie the Black Death and other tarpon flies in a range of sizes,
although many guides prefer smaller flies for attracting these large fish.

In addition to tying the tail using saddle hackles, you may substitute with
a black rabbit Zonker strip. This is easy to tie to the hook, and the soft fur
flows in the water when retrieving the fly. Also, rather than using squirrel
tail hair for the collar, substitute with red or black saddle hackle.

Play around with different materials and dark colors, and create your
own version of the Black Death. Just be sure to release the tarpon alive!

Devil's Daughter

Hook: Tiemco TMC811S or Daiichi 2546, size 1 or 1/0.
Thread: Black Danville 210 denier.
Tail: Peacock herl and black ostrich plume.
Body: Black marabou plumes.
Head: Black deer body hair, spun on the hook and clipped to shape like a Muddler Minnow.

MOST EXPERIENCED TARPON ANGLERS SAY YOU MUST have patterns tied in a variety of basic colors: bright flies (white chartreuse, and yellow) for fishing on bright days and over light-colored flats, and at least one black pattern for dark days or those times when the fish show no interest in brighter flies. This approach makes a lot of sense, especially for newer tarpon fishermen filling their first box of flies: keep it simple and you'll increase your odds of success.

The very best tarpon anglers also recommend flies that "push" water. The gentle disturbance created by a fly moving through the water on the retrieve mimics the vibrations of a feeling baitfish. Tarpon and other game-fish detect these vibrations through their lateral lines which helps them home in on the fly. The head on the Devil's Daughter, which is deer hair spun and clipped to resemble the head of a Muddler Minnow, does a fine job of pushing water. And the fly's black color is ideal for anchoring the dark end of your fly box.

Although the original Devil's Daughter is tied in black, you can use the basic design to create tarpon flies in a variety of other colors. Retain the deer-hair head, but tie the fly in any color you wish using hackles. A head of natural-colored deer hair and white feathers for the wing would be especially effective.

White Noise

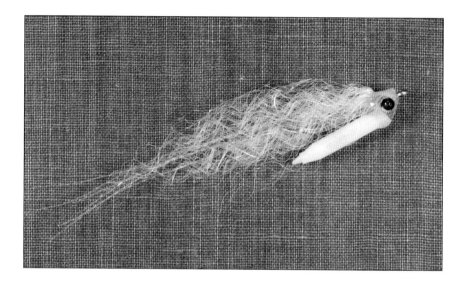

Hook: Tiemco TMC811S or Daiichi 2546, size 1 or 2.
Thread: Clear monofilament.
Body: Steve Farrar's SF Flash Blend (white) and pearl UV Krystal Flash.
Eyes: Large black plastic dumbbell.
Head: Five-minute epoxy or light-cured acrylic.
Rattle: Glow-in-the-dark plastic worm rattle.

ACCORDING TO FLY-DESIGNER DREW CHICONE, HE CAME up with idea for the White Noise while fishing the beaches of Captiva. All the bait he was encountering appears semi-translucent, and he wanted a pattern to match. Steve Farrar's SF Flash Blend, with a few sprigs of UV Krystal Flash, comprise the wispy now-you-see-it, now-you-don't body of the fly. The White Noise is not an exact imitation of any particular form of bait; it might resemble many things predator fish will eat.

In addition to designing a very sparse fly, Drew wanted his new pattern to make a little noise to attract fish. He had not tied many flies containing rattles because most were glass; Drew says that glass rattles look too fragile, and they are too hard to tie to a hook. Drew uses a plastic worm rattle in the White Noise, which is far more durable and easy to secure to the fly. Do rattles really work on fishing flies? Dr. David Ross, of Woods Hole Oceano-graphic Institution and a fly-fishing fanatic, insists rattles improve many flies and help catch fish. He tells stories of seeing fish turn and travel great distances to locate patterns containing rattles.

Tie and fish the White Noise and judge for yourself. Or, add rattles to some of your favorite patterns and see if they catch more fish. I'll enjoy hearing the results of your experiments.

Asphyxiator

Hook: Daiichi 2546, size 4 or 2.
Thread: Black 6/0.
Tail: Four grizzly hackles and two strands of root beer Krystal Flash.
Body: Two grizzly hackles.
Eyes: Medium copper bead chain.

ARE YOU NEW TO TYING FLIES? DO YOU WANT A SIMPLE pattern for learning the basics of starting the thread and securing basic materials to the hook? The Asphyxiator is the fly for you.

Check out the list of tying materials: a hook, thread, hackles, flash material, and bead-chain eyes. That's it! For about $20 you can get enough ingredients to fill a fly box full of fish-catching flies. And, you can gradually make this pattern in other colors to meet a wide range of fishing situations.

I always recommend that new tiers start with three or four patterns that catch fish in their local waters. Become an expert in tying those flies and gain confidence that your handiwork will really catch fish. Add new patterns slowly and you will reduce the amount of money you spend on your new hobby. You will also discover that you can use many of the materials you have to tie other flies.

In this case, the Daiichi 2546 is an ordinary hook suitable for tying dozens of different flies. A spool of black thread is one of the most generic materials and is called for in hundreds of pattern recipes. Grizzly hackles are as common to fly tying as chickens are to barnyards. Krystal Flash and bead-chain eyes are also popular ingredients.

Drew Chicone's Asphyxiator is a great first fly.

Disco Shrimp

Hook: Mustad 34011 or a similar long-shank saltwater hook, size 1 or 2.
Thread: Brown Danville 210 denier.
Head: Red fox tail hair.
Antennae: Peacock Krystal Flash.
Eyes: Melted monofilament.
Legs: Tan rubber legs.
Body: Golden brown Ice Dub.
Back: Tan 2-millimeter-thick closed-cell foam.
Rattle: Plastic worm rattle.
Tail: Two 4-millimeter gold sequins.

MOST ANGLERS THINK THAT SHRIMP IMITATIONS ARE always subsurface patterns, but nothing is further from the case. I have caught baby tarpon in the canals of the Florida Keys using topwater shrimp imitations. This is especially fun sport in the evening when the tarpon are feeding on real shrimp under street lights and porch lamps. Cast your fly in the vicinity of feeding fish, let it rest for a few moments, and then impart a slow, chugging retrieve. It might take several casts, but a tarpon will eventually take your fly.

Of course, topwater patterns are used for catching a great many species of fish. Drew Chicone designed his Disco Shrimp for catching mangrove snapper, but it will also catch striped bass and more.

The Disco Shrimp has two features that create fish-enticing noise. First, before tying the fly, slip two 4-millimeter gold sequins on the hook and behind the eye. When drawn through the water, the sequins act like a tiny popping head. Second, a plastic worm rattle is tied to the end of the hook shank and shrouded under the fox fur. When you shake the Disco Shrimp in your hand, you can feel the rattle jingling. Both of these great features get the attention of the fish.

Lefty's Deceiver

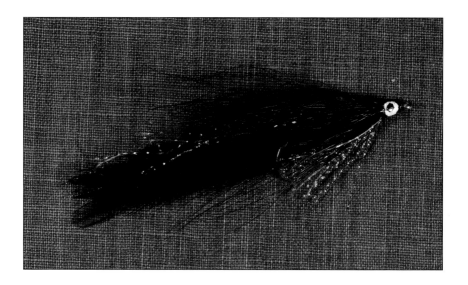

Hook: Regular saltwater hook, sizes 8 to 2/0.
Thread: Size 3/0.
Tail: Saddle hackles with strands of your favorite flash material.
Body: Flat silver tinsel.
Back: Bucktail.
Belly: Bucktail.
Eyes: Painted or adhesive eyes coated with epoxy.

FLY-FISHING LEGEND LEFTY KREH DESIGNED HIS LEFTY'S Deceiver many years ago. Thousands of anglers use this great pattern to catch a wide variety of fish. If you tie your own flies, you must put Lefty's Deceiver on your list of patterns.

Tie Lefty's Deceiver in a range of sizes and colors. The most popular color combinations are blue/white, olive/white, and chartreuse/white; an all-white Deceiver is also a favored fly. Some anglers also carry a few black Deceivers for fishing on cloudy days; the theory is that a dark pattern presents a better silhouette for the fish to spot the fly.

Adding a few strands of Krystal Flash or Flashabou gives the Deceiver a little fish-attracting twinkle. And when tying the tail, try using saddle hackles that have somewhat stiff quills; this will help prevent the feathers from twisting around the bend of the hook when casting.

If you wish to add eyes to your Deceiver, tie the fly using size 3/0 thread; this will allow you to quickly wrap a larger head as a base for the eyes. You can make the eyes using enamel paint, or use small adhesive eyes. Coat the eyes with thick head cement or epoxy.

Bendback

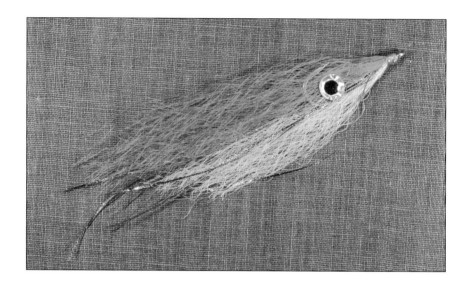

Hook: Long-shank saltwater hook, sizes 4 to 2/0.
Thread: Size 3/0.
Body: Ultra Wire, tinsel, or Mylar tubing.
Wing: Bucktail, FisHair, or your choice of wing material.
Flash material: Flashabou, Krystal Flash, or your choice of flash material.
Eyes: Enamel paint or holographic eyes glued to the sides of the head.

GO ONLINE AND SEARCH FOR THE BENDBACK AND YOU'LL be blown away by the wide variety of flies tied using this format. When it was first created, the Bendback was very simple: a tinsel body, bucktail wing, and thread head. Today, inventive tiers convert many of their favorite patterns into Bendbacks.

The term "bendback" refers to the shape of the hook, not the materials used to tie the fly. The hook is bent up slightly about one-third of an inch from the eye. Place the altered hook in the vise with the point on top and tie the pattern. The altered shape of the hook and the full wing encourage the fly to fish with the point on top so it does not snag on rocks and weeds.

Once upon a time, Mustad manufactured hooks for tying Bendbacks, but they have been discontinued. You can easily bend a stainless steel hook into the proper shape using small pliers, and experiment with hooks of various degrees of bend. Another option, overlooked by many fly tiers, is hooks designed for rigging plastic worms when fishing for freshwater bass. I tie Bendbacks, and simply bend my hooks to shape.

Whether you fish marl flats for redfish or rocky outcroppings for striped bass and bluefish, use Bendbacks to prevent snagging the bottom and to keep fishing.

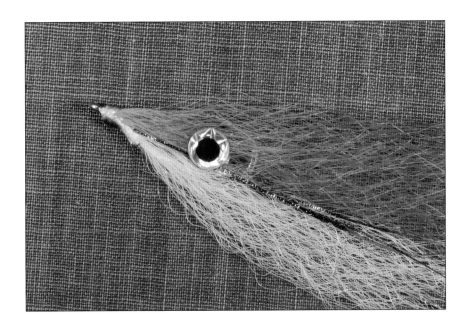

Flashtail Clouser Minnow

Hook: Targus 9413 or TFS 5444 60-degree bent-shank jig hook, size 2/0.

Thread: White Danville Fly Master Plus and red Fly Masters Plus.

Eyes: Spirit River Real Eyes Plus, 7/32-inch, nickel/yellow.

Flashtail: Silver and pearl Flashabou.

Tail: White bucktail and white Slinky Flash.

Side flash: Silver and pearl Flashabou.

Belly: White bucktail and white Slinky Flash.

Wing: White bucktail, white Slinky Flash, chartreuse Slinky Flash, and chartreuse bucktail.

Topping: Light blue Krystal Flash.

BOB CLOUSER'S FAMOUS CLOUSER MINNOW—THE ORIGINAL
version or the Flashtail Clouser Minnow—has to be included on many top-10
lists of saltwater patterns. Like many great flies, the Clouser Minnow offers a
base for experimenting and making innovative modifications. Striper-fishing
guru Dan Blanton's Flashtail Whistler, an outgrowth of the original Whistler, is a
wonderful example. In fact, after tying his Flashtail Whistler, he quickly recommended adding flashtails to the Clouser Minnow, Lefty's Deceiver, and many
other flies. The synthetic materials brightened these patterns and, under the
right conditions, made them more effective.

The weighted Flashtail Clouser Minnow cuts through heavy currents
to reach fish holding in eddies and seams. You can modify the weight of
the fly when selecting dumbbell eyes and materials. The Flashtail Clouser
Minnow, with the dumbbell placed near the hook eye, bobs up and down
in the water like a jig. Tying the fly to your leader using a loop knot will
accentuate this jigging action.

Flashtail Whistler

Hook: Gamakatsu 29111-25 or an equivalent, sizes 1/0 to 4/0.

Thread: Clear medium monofilament or chartreuse Danville Flat Waxed Nylon.

Eyes: Extra-large silver bead chain.

Weight: Size .030-inch lead or nontoxic wire.

Flashtail and side flash: Pearl Flashabou.

Tail: White, chartreuse, and misty blue H2O SF Flash Blend.

Wing: White H2O SF Flash Blend.

Topping: Light blue Krystal Flash.

Collar: Medium red Vernille.

Hackle: White medium saddle or large neck hackles.

DAN BLANTON TIED THE WHISTLER IN THE 1960S TO IMITATE a bucktail jig, the most effective striped bass lure ever created. Dan's first Whistlers were pretty dull, tied using only bucktail and feathers. But, in the early 1970s, Dan added Mylar tinsel and eventually Flashabou to the tail of Whistler, and the pattern quickly became a fish-catching sensation.

"Flashtails on flies are like the tail of a comet or the flaming exhaust of a rocket heading into orbit on a black night," Dan once wrote.

In addition to the Flashtail, Dan added synthetic body materials and a 60-degree jig hook. All these synthetic materials are easy to use, and once you find a winning color combination, you can always find the exact same materials in the fly shop. And, a Flashtail Whistler is a very durable pattern.

A Flashtail Whistler pushes water, making it especially effective for attracting fish in stained conditions. Tie it to imitate the color of local prey or in brighter hues as an attractor pattern; it's hard to avoid adding chartreuse to the Flashtail Whistler. You can also tie Dan's pattern with more translucent synthetic materials for fishing in the clearer water conditions common in the Southeast.

Purple Tide Slave

Hook: Gamakatsu SC-15, size 1/0.

Thread: Purple 3/0.

Weight: Large tungsten dumbbell painted purple.

Mouth parts: Fluorescent fire orange or root beer Krystal Flash.

Eyes: Extra-large EP Crab/Shrimp Eyes.

Legs: Purple/pumpkin Fly Enhancer Legs.

Body: Sand EP Foxy Bush and tan arctic fox fur.

Extras: Clear Cure Goo Hydro and Sally Hansen Miracle Gel Nail Polish—Too Haute 520.

A GREAT FISH-CATCHING FLY IS A BLEND OF SEVERAL important elements. First, the pattern must reach the correct depth in the water column; too high or too low, and fish might miss seeing it or they might be locked into feeding on bait at a different depth. Size is also an important consideration; typically, a fly can be a size or two smaller than the real bait, but fish often pass on a fly that is too large. Color is sometimes critical, although I have played with the idea of tying all my flies in chartreuse; I suspect I wouldn't catch fewer fish, and there are times I might actually catch more. And last, but hardly least, a good fly creates a natural swimming or moving action in the water when retrieved. The Tide Slave, which is tied using several soft flowing materials, has terrific swimming action when moving through the water.

This slightly larger Tide Slave, dressed on a size 1/0 hook, is a good choice when fishing for permit. The dumbbell eyes will help the fly sink quickly to the right depth before the fish turn and swim in a new direction. Scale the Tide Slave down to size 4 or 2, and substitute with bead-chain eyes, and you'll have a first-rate bonefish fly.

Green Deceiver

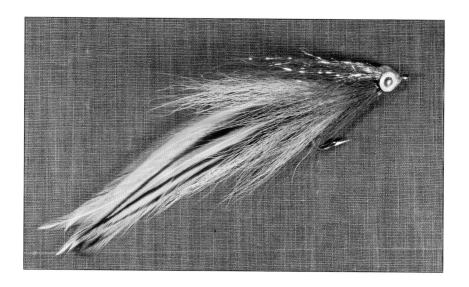

Hook: Regular saltwater hook, size 2/0 or 4/0.
Thread: Clear monofilament.
Tail: White and chartreuse saddle hackles.
Body: White, chartreuse, and olive bucktail.
Back: Green thin Flashabou or a similar material.
Eyes: Medium pearl 3-D eyes.

THIS FLY, TIED BY JERE HALDEMANN, WON THE SALTWATER
category in the fly-tying contest held at the annual 2014 International Fly
Tying Symposium.

Every November, tiers gather outside New York City in Somerset, New
Jersey, to share their latest flies and newest tying techniques. A fly-tying
contest is one of the features of the Symposium. Participants to the contest
do not have to be present to win, so flies arrive from around the world. The
judges are many of the tiers in attendance, which has included Bob Popovics, Bob Clouser, Jay "Fishy" Fullum, Gary Borger, and many other famous
anglers. These esteemed judges selected Haldemann's Green Deceiver as the
winner.

In addition to being a first-rate example of a Deceiver, Haldemann's
Green Deceiver points to the importance of blending colors. Sure, there are
plenty of solid-color flies—white, chartreuse, black, and more—and they all
catch fish. But, nothing in nature is a solid color. Whether for camouflage
or perhaps to attract a mate, most fish, birds, and other forms of wildlife are
many colors. This Green Deceiver is a wonderful blend of colors that give
it the general appearance of a real baitfish.

Think about blending colors when tying flies. Select contrasting shades
of feathers and furs and your flies will look more lifelike.

Tabory's Snake Fly

Hook: Varivas 990S or a similar hook, size 2/0 or 3/0.
Thread: White 3/0.
Tail: White, pink and olive ostrich herl, and pearl Flashabou.
Head: White deer hair.
Eyes: Doll eyes or a weighted dumbbell.

LOU TABORY ROCKED THE FLY-FISHING WORLD IN 1992 when he published his book *Inshore Fly Fishing*. Although anglers had trekked the coasts for years in search of striped bass, bluefish, and other favorite gamefish, Lou laid all the secrets bare: tackle selection, rigging, fishing techniques, and flies. Thousands of fly fishermen discovered a new way to enjoy their sport. As a result of this interest, tackle manufacturers introduced new rods, reels, and lines, and fly tiers started making new patterns. Because of this profound impact, one angler from the New Jersey Shore said that Lou Tabory was saltwater fly-fishing's version of Theodore Gordon.

Tabory introduced this pattern, called the Snake Fly, in *Inshore Fly Fishing*. Fish this pattern near the surface using a floating line, with a sinking-tip, or a full sinking line to reach deeper into the water column. The version of the Snake Fly we see here is tied using metal dumbbell eyes to add weight and swim deep, but you can also glue lightweight 3-D or small doll eyes to the top of the clipped deer-hair head.

The broad head will push water and help the fish find the fly. In addition to white, tie Tabory's Snake Fly in any of your favorite fish-catching colors. And, rather than constructing the tail using fragile ostrich herl, substitute with bucktail.

Tarpon Toad

Hook: Regular saltwater hook, size 2/0.
Thread: Black 3/0.
Tail: Black marabou.
Head: Red rug yarn.
Eyes: Black plastic dumbbell.

THE TARPON TOAD, SOMETIMES CALLED SIMPLY "THE TOAD," is based on Del Brown's famous permit fly called the Merkin. Del tied pieces of stiff rug yarn perpendicular to the hook shank to create the oval body of a crab. This pattern has become a universal hit, and other tiers have created new patterns using this design.

Gary Merriman created the Tarpon Toad in the 1990s using Brown's idea for making the body of his fly. Gary's goal when designing the Tarpon Toad was to create a pattern that would remain suspended higher in the water column and have a lot of natural swimming action. Although the original Tarpon Toad was tied using light-colored yellow materials, you can make this pattern in any colors you wish. Here we see a black-and-red version of the fly which is perfect for when you want to fish with a dark-colored fly.

Two versions of the Tarpon Toad have evolved over the years. The original had a tail tied using a rabbit Zonker strip; this style of pattern is still very popular. The second, which we see here, omits the Zonker strip. The fluffy marabou tail still imparts a lot of swimming action, and there is no long rabbit strip to foul around the hook while casting.

Cyclops

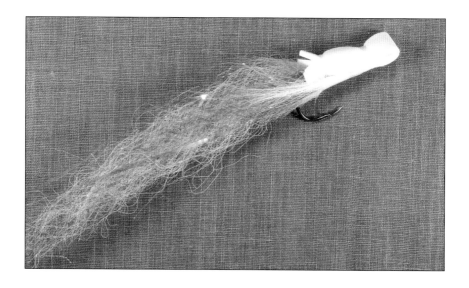

Hook: Regular saltwater, size 1/0.
Thread: White 3/0.
Tail: White and blue Big Fly Fiber, and red, white, and blue calftail or a substitute.
Eye: Adhesive eye.

MATT RAMSEY, WHO DESIGNS FLIES FOR UMPQUA FEATHER
Merchants, created this cool topwater pattern called Cyclops. The Cyclops
is a slider and is perfect for casting to striped bass when they are feeding on
baitfish near the surface of the water. It is also simple to make and perfect
for new tiers looking for their first topwater fly.

Big Fly Fiber is a long crinkled hair material suitable for making very
large flies. It comes in a rainbow of colors, so you can tie Cyclops to suit
your mode as well as the mode of the fish. Because of its crinkled nature,
you can tie a full-bodied fly using only a small bunch of material.

Matt and his fishing partner, Scott Nelson, own an outfitting business
called Two Dudes Flyfishing, in Eugene, Oregon. Matt says he created the
Cyclops for catching taimen in Mongolia. Taimen are the world's largest sal-
monid. The Cyclops was a hit for catching those strong fish, but the Cyclops
had obvious application for saltwater fly fishing.

The head of the fly is folded closed-cell foam. The tail of the Cyclops
sinks slightly into the surface film, but the foam head remains above the
surface. Place a single eye on the bottom of the head so that it faces down,
making the fly simulate a wounded baitfish lying on the surface. Coat the
bottom of the head with head cement to seal the eye in place.

Rattle Rouser

Hook: Eagle Claw 413, sizes 2 to 3/0.
Thread: Black 3/0.
Body: Pearl Mylar tubing.
Rattle: Large glass rattle.
Wing: Big Fly Fiber, Super Hair, or your favorite synthetic hair material, and strands of Flashabou or a substitute.
Eyes: Large silver 3-D eyes.

ACCORDING TO MY RESEARCH, EXPERT FLY DESIGNER Kirk Dietrich, of Louisiana, created the Rattle Rouser. It is a fine searching pattern although you can tie it in colors to match most of our favorite large baitfish: mackerel, bunker, herring, and more. Substitute colors of materials and use waterproof pens to add barring and other markings to imitate all these species of prey.

The Eagle Claw 413 is an economical jig hook suitable for use in salt water. This heavy-wire hook comes with Eagle Claw's Seaguard finish, which protects the hook and prevents it from corroding. The shank is bent at a 60-degree angle near the hook eye. This hook works better than a jig hook bent at a 90-degree angle for a streamer such as the Rattle Rouser. The fly swims through the water more naturally yet the hook point still remains on top.

The glass rattle, inserted in the Mylar tubing, appears as a belly on the fly and gets the fishes' attention. Many anglers argue that a fly containing a rattle catches more fish. Tie a few Rattle Rousers and see if you catch more fish.

The sealed glass rattle adds buoyancy to the belly of the fly. Although the shape of the jig hook forces the fly to ride with the hook point on top, the rattle encourages the fly to flip over. Slip a couple of BBs in the Mylar tubing before adding the rattle. This small amount of ballast keeps the Rattle Rouser tracking true through the water.

Buzzi's Painted Poppers

Hook: 4X- or 6X-longer saltwater hook in your choice of sizes.
Body: Pre-formed foam popper. Wrap the hook shank with thread, and then glue the body in place using epoxy. Paint the body using the Copic Airbrush System.
Tail: Feathers, fur, or your favorite tail materials.
Eyes: Paint or adhesive.

POPPERS ARE SOME OF OUR FAVORITE TOPWATER FLIES. Poppers are commonly used for catching striped bass, bluefish, and other aggressive meat-eating fish, but some anglers use smaller poppers for catching redfish and even sea trout. The key to catching reds and "specks" with a popper is not to spook the fish, so retrieve the fly gently, creating only a very light chucking sound.

All fly shops carry a selection of poppers, or you can make your own. Typically, however, homemade poppers look a little boring; they usually have rough bodies and are solid colors. Popper-making guru Brad Buzzi creates poppers complete with painted scales and other patterns that you commonly find only on manufactured lures. While the fish don't care about the finished appearance of a popper, he is a master at crafting poppers that appeal to anglers.

Brad paints the bodies of his flies using the Copic Airbrush System, which you can find in almost any well-stocked crafts store, online, and in a few fly shops. The Copic airbrush uses permanent-marker ink, which comes in dozens of colors. If you paint a large number of poppers, you can purchase marker refills suitable for coloring dozens of flies; after the initial investment for the airbrush, you can paint flies for just a few cents apiece.

Brad first sprays the base colors on the body (working from light to dark), and then allows the ink to dry. Next, he wraps nylon screen or netting on the body as a mask and paints the popper with a contrasting color. Removing the netting reveals wonderful scales. Finally, Brad adds eyes, seals the body with thirty-minute epoxy, and ties the tail. The results are outstanding, and this is something you can do—really!

Clouser Minnow

Hook: Long-shank saltwater hook, sizes 8 to 2/0.
Weight: Dumbbell or bead chain.
Thread: Your choice of color, size 3/0.
Body: Flat silver or pearl tinsel.
Wing: Bucktail or your favorite fine-fibered synthetic hair, your choice of colors.

THE CLOUSER MINNOW HAS BEEN ONE OF OUR MOST popular streamers for many years. Born on Pennsylvania's Susquehanna River for catching smallmouth bass, it quickly migrated to the salt and became a favorite pattern for catching striped bass, bluefish, sea trout, and a wide variety of other species.

A lot of anglers overlook the Clouser Minnow as a worthy fly for catching wary flats fish such as bonefish, permit, and redfish. I always carry Clouser Minnows tied on size 8 hooks with small bead-chain eyes and chartreuse craft-fur wings; more than one shallow-water guide has plucked this pattern out of my fly box and said, "Try this first."

Several years ago, while visiting Florida to attend a wedding, I took off for an afternoon to fish Indian River Lagoon with Captain John Kumiski. We caught several ladyfish and crevalle jacks, and near the end of the day, John motored us across the lagoon to a flats where he thought we'd have a shot at redfish. Sure enough, within just a few minutes, we spotted three reds pushing water and heading our way. I cast one of those lightweight flies well ahead of the fish and let it sink. Finally, as the redfish moved within three feet of my fly, I tightened the line and gently lifted it from the sandy bottom. The slight movement triggered the fish to attack: they burst forward and one snatched the fly. I repeated this tactic several more times that day and caught half a dozen powerful redfish.

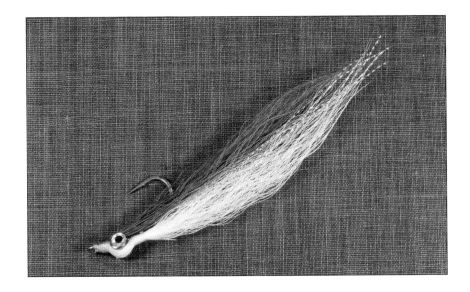

Apte Tarpon Fly

Hook: Long-shank saltewater hook, sizes 6 to 1/0.
Thread: Orange 3/0.
Tail: Orange and yellow saddle hackles.
Collar: Orange saddle hackle.
Body: Orange tying thread.

THE LEGENDARY STU APTE, ONE OF OUR GREATEST TARPON fly anglers, once wrote: "A typical tarpon fishing scenario might have you standing on a casting platform for hours, holding your rod with one hand, the fly in the fingers of your other hand, and waiting for that one opportunity. All of the sudden the guide excitedly whispers, 'There she is . . . 11 o'clock . . . sixty feet. Make the cast! Drop it right in front of her face. Now! NOW!'"

No one knows tarpon fishing better than Stu. He has spent untold thousands of hours pursuing trophy tarpon, and he has caught hundreds of these fish. In fact, Stu has landed more tarpon than most avid saltwater anglers see in a lifetime.

The Apte Tarpon Fly is a simple concoction: hook, thread, and hackles. Some anglers say that the pattern's characteristic long snout simulates a needlefish, and the long, feathered tail creates excellent swimming action. One of the keys of the Apte Tarpon fly is the heavy hackle collar tied at the end of the hook shank. The thick collar "pushes" water when the pattern is stripped through the water, creating a disturbance that helps a tarpon locate the fly.

The classic Apte Tarpon Fly, which was featured on a US postage stamp, is tied in orange and yellow. Many knowledgeable anglers choose this version on sunny days and when fishing over bright flats. Use this pattern as a model, but change colors to create a fly box full of fish-catching patterns for meeting any fishing condition.

Remember that fishing for trophy tarpon is not about casting; instead, you will spend a great deal of time searching the water looking for a big fish to slide within casting range. You will want a fly you can depend on. The Apte Tarpon Fly is a time-honored pattern that you will want in your fishing kit for your next trip to the flats.

Caloosahatchee Cannibal

Hook: Gamakatsu SC-15, size 2/0.
Thread: Clear monofilament.
Belly: White saltwater yak hair and pearl Wing N' Flash.
Back: White, tan, and yellow saltwater yak hair.
Eyes: 8-millimeter clear doll eyes.

THE CALOOSAHATCHEE RIVER IS ON THE GULF COAST IN southwest Florida. The mouth of the river, near Fort Myers, Cape Coral, and Sanibel Island, has long been a prime fishing destination. In *The Book of the Tarpon*, which was written in the early part of the twentieth century, early angling authority A. W. Dimock describes fishing the Caloosahatchee River. *The Book of the Tarpon* is considered the first volume devoted to this magnificent game fish.

Although the river has changed since Dimock fished there, it is still considered a prime tarpon destination; some anglers consider it the most consistent producer of tarpon in Lee County, Florida. In addition to tarpon, the area's mangroves hold snook. Tie Drew Chicone's Caloosahatchee Cannibal, and a variety of similar flies, and you'll surely enjoy some fine fishing. And be sure to pack some small crab imitations and other small patterns for catching redfish and sea trout.

There are plenty of fine guides in the area, and you'll easily find lodging in Fort Myers or Cape Coral. If you prefer roughing it, check out Caloosahatchee Regional Park, which is operated by Lee County Parks & Recreation. The park offers inexpensive camping, and you're just a short drive from good fishing.

The water in the Caloosahatchee River is somewhat stained. The tall Caloosahatchee Cannibal, which is a general baitfish imitation, pushes water so hungry fish can easily locate the fly.

Captiva Cannibal

Hook: Gamakatsu SC-15, size 2/0.
Thread: Monofilament.
Belly: White saltwater yak hair and pearl Wing N' Flash.
Back: White, gray, tan, and turquoise saltwater yak hair, and silver Wing N' Flash.
Eyes: 8-millimeter clear doll eyes.

NOTHING EVER STAYS THE SAME, AND THIS IS ESPECIALLY true along the storm-swept Florida Coast. Strong winds, hurricanes, and tidal surges are continually changing the coastline. For example, Captiva Island was part of neighboring Sanibel Island to the southeast. In 1926, a hurricane's storm surge created a new channel, separating Captiva from Sanibel. And North Captiva Island was severed from Captiva during a hurricane in 1921, creating Redfish Pass. (Hmm, wonder how it got its name?) Captiva is a barrier island to Pine Island, which was once surely part of the mainland.

All of these islands contain flats, mangroves, and backchannels, the kinds of places that hold fish. Hire a guide and his boat if you are new to the area; there are plenty of expert anglers who can show you the best fishing. Or, if you like to explore and want to plan your own trip, take or rent a kayak to access many miles of fine fishing.

The Captiva Cannibal is the cousin to the Caloosahatchee Cannibal. Make both patterns using the same tying methods, just alter the colors of the materials used in constructing the backs and bellies. Drew Chicone says he ties the Captiva Cannibal for fishing the turquois-colored water surrounding the island. This is a great fishing destination; you could spend a week there and never get bored.

Crease Fly

Hook: Long-shank saltwater hook, sizes 4 to 2/0.
Thread: Your choice of color, size A.
Tail: Bucktail and Krystal Flash, your choice of colors.
Body: Closed-cell foam, your choice of color.
Eyes: Gold or silver adhesive eyes.

CAPTAIN JOE BLADOS, OF GREENPORT, NEW YORK, CREATED
the innovative Crease Fly. Captain Blados designed the Crease Fly to catch
the striped bass, bluefish, and other species that visit Long Island every
summer. The pattern is a lightweight, easy-to-cast alternative to a popper.
The narrow profile slices through the air, yet the fly, with its cupped face
makes a lot of commotion on the surface of the water when retrieving
the fly.

The Crease Fly is fun and easy to make. First tie the tail using bucktail in
your choice of colors. Include a few sprigs of Krystal Flash to add a twinkle to the tail when the fly is resting on the water. The butt end of the tail
should extend along the entire hook shank to create a solid base for gluing
on the foam body.

The body of the Crease Fly is thin closed-cell foam folded and glued to
the hook using superglue. Cut the foam to shape using heavy hobby scissors,
not fine fly-tying scissors. Check out the photo of the Crease Fly; use that
as a guide when shaping the foam for your flies. A company called River
Roads Creations offers a set of cutters, similar to cookie cutters, designed to
punch out the bodies of foam Crease Flies.

After gluing the body of the Crease Fly to the hook, you may add
eyes and color the foam. Coating the finished fly with epoxy dramatically
increases the durability of the finished pattern, and you can use one fly to
catch dozens of fish.

Blonde

Hook: Regular saltwater hook, sizes 8 to 2/0.
Thread: Black 6/0.
Tail: Bucktail.
Body: Flat, round, or braided tinsel.
Wing: Bucktail.
Note: Select bucktail in the colors of your choice.

THE BLONDE IS A TRUE FLY-FISHING CLASSIC. GENERALLY credited to famed angler and author Joe Brooks, Colonel Joseph Bates, a serious student of the history of flies and fly fishing, says both Brooks and Homer Rhode Jr., created the Blonde. Of course, the Blonde is such an incredibly simple fly that I am sure many tiers, working independently, made the same type of basic pattern; what's hard about tying a bucktail wing and tail to a hook?

In 1963, Brooks wrote an article for *Outdoor Life* about a fishing trip he took to Argentina. He said, "This was my first trip to Argentina, back in 1955. Packing my tackle at home I kept thinking about the 10, 12, 14 and even 20-pound brown trout that Jorge Donovan had told me were in the Argentine rivers. Remembering that old theory that a big trout likes a big mouthful, I had reached into my salt-water tackle box and picked out a handful of 'blonde' flies—big, white bucktails that I used for striped bass."

The Blonde is still a great pattern for catching striped bass, but it is also a terrific choice for bluefish and other toothy species that shed flies; tying a Blonde takes only a couple of minutes and the materials are inexpensive, so you'll shed no tears if the fish destroy a couple of flies.

The name of the fly comes from the fact that the Blonde was originally tied in white, cream, and pale yellow, but you may use any colors you like— red, olive, black, tan, and more. The Blonde is a particularly fine fly for new tiers; it requires only the most basic skills to make.

Homer Rhode
Tarpon Fly

Hook: Regular-length saltwater hook, sizes 1/0 to 3/0.
Thread: Black 3/0.
Wing: Grizzly, white, and yellow saddle hackles, or in the colors of your choice.
Collar: White and yellow saddle hackles, or in the colors of your choice.

WITH THE EVOLUTION OF NEW TACKLE, FISHING FOR tarpon grew in popularity. For some anglers, it is their passion; they spend almost all their time on the water searching for these mighty fish. Fiberglass and then graphite rods, and the development of nylon and fluorocarbon leaders, made it possible to hook and hold large tarpon. Even before these remarkable pieces of tackle were available, anglers competed to see who could land the biggest tarpon.

The Miami Beach Rod and Reel Club started the Metropolitan Miami Fishing Tournament in 1935. The purpose of this fly-fishing event was to encourage tourism and fishing in South Florida. In 1940, Howard Bonbright set the tournament record for tarpon at 36.5 pounds, but in 1952, H. K. Atkins set a new tournament record with a tarpon weighing 51.8 pounds. Although they were a long way from catching 100-pound-plus freight-train tarpon, the hunt was on for trophy fish.

Homer Rhode was an early champion of catching tarpon on flies. He was a ranger in Everglades National Park, and was catching bonefish and permit on flies in the 1930s. This fly is considered the forerunner of the Seaducer series of patterns.

Tie the hackle collar of the Homer Rhode Tarpon Fly full so it "pushes" water when stripped on the retrieve. Many experienced anglers swear that this sets off subtle vibrations through the water that help the fish locate the fly. Also notice that this pattern is tied in the classic tarpon-fly format with a small bare space behind the eye for tying the fly to the leader.

Joe Brooks Tarpon Fly

Hook: Your favorite brand of regular-length saltwater hook, sizes 1/0 to 3/0.
Thread: Red 3/0.
Wing: White saddle hackles.
Collar: Red marabou.

SOME KNOWLEDGEABLE ANGLERS CONSIDER JOE BROOKS the father of modern fly fishing. You've never head of him? Well, Joe died in 1972 while on a fishing trip to the Yellowstone Country, and so he has become overlooked by many younger anglers. Today, most anglers would mention Lefty Kreh as our most significant fly fisherman, but even the great Lefty wrote, "Joe Brooks had the biggest influence on me; he got me into writing and got me into fly fishing. He got me interested in salt water fishing."

Brooks was a worldwide ambassador for all forms of angling, and trekked across the globe in search of good fishing. He was an author and tackle innovator. He also designed very simple yet effective flies. For example, the Blonde, a simple pattern we are including in this book, is a fly even novice tiers can quickly make. The Joe Brooks Tarpon Fly is another simple pattern you will want to add to your fishing kit.

The Joe Brooks Tarpon Fly helped shape what we think of as the classic-fly form. The long tail hackles are tied splayed near the end of the hook shank, and the thread nose occupies the middle one-third of the shank; there is a bare space behind the eye for tying the fly to the leader using a turle knot. Tie the collar using a small marabou feather rather than hackle. The hackle is full enough to "push" water on the calm tarpon flats and gives the fly a pulsating, lifelike swimming action.

Billy Pate Homassasa Tarpon Fly

Hook: Your favorite brand of regular-length, heavy-wire saltwater hook, sizes 2/0 and 3/0.

Thread: Size 3/0.

Wing: Saddle hackles in your choice of colors.

Collar: Bucktail in your choice of colors.

Eyes: Medium chrome dumbbell.

Note: Here's another pattern for fishing very deep.

BILLY PATE WAS ONE OF THE LEADERS IN THE EVOLUTION of fly fishing for tarpon. In 1982, he set a world record by boating a fish weighing 188 pounds using a 16-pound-test tippet. He caught that fish in Homassasa, Florida, and for almost twenty years, anglers gathered in those storied waters to try to break his record. In addition to this impressive record, Pate was also the first angler to catch all four species of marlin—black, blue, white, and striped—using a fly rod. These feats, and more, made him a big-game fly-fishing legend.

Pate, who passed away in 2011 at the age of eighty, was a much beloved figure in the fly-fishing world. He was inducted into the Fishing Hall of Fame at the International Gamefish Association, and was a member of the Everglades Protection Association, Trout Unlimited, the Bonefish & Tarpon Trust, the Don Hawley Foundation, the Miami Beach Rod and Reel Club, and the Islamorada Fishing Club. Billy spent many years working in the carpet business, and eventually he and Captain George Hommell founded a terrific business called World Wide Sportsman, in Islamorada, Florida. Billy and George eventually sold the business to Pro Bass Shops, but you can still stop at World Wide Sportsman when passing through Islamorada.

His Homassasa Tarpon Fly is tied using a medium chrome dumbbell. The dumbbell, perched on the top of the hook shank, adds a small amount of weight to the fly which makes it ideal for casting to fish lying in deeper water.

Gurgler

Hook: Long-shank saltwater hook, sizes 2 to 2/0.
Thread: Size 3/0.
Tail: Bucktail or your favorite long hair and strands of Krystal Flash, Flashabou, or another brand of flash material.
Body: Krystal Chenille.
Body hackle: Saddle hackle.
Back: Closed-cell foam.

THE GURGLER MAY BE THE BEST-KNOWN PATTERN designed by the late Jack Gartside.

Jack was an entertaining figure at almost all of the East Coast fly-fishing shows. He was also a very talented pattern designer. His specialty was creating fish-catching flies using a minimum number of ingredients. The Gurgler is a great example of his ingenuity.

The Gurgler is one of the most popular floating saltwater flies ever devised. It is very easy to tie, and although the body is foam, it is surprisingly durable. A sharp-toothed bluefish might destroy a Gurgler, but you can catch a couple dozen striped bass using the same fly. In fact, I have several Gurglers in my fly box all sporting tags of monofilament on the hook eyes; I used these flies, and they are all in good enough condition to use again in the future.

Tie the Gurgler in a variety of sizes and colors. A yellow or orange Gurgler is easy to see on the surface of the water when the fly is at rest.

Sometimes a popper makes too much noise, especially when fishing on the flats or in shallow water. A Gurgler, however, makes a more subtle noise. The gentle gurgling sound attracts rather than repels fish. Tie or purchase a few Gurglers, and they will quickly become an important part of your fishing kit.

FishHead

Hook: Mustad 34007, 3407DT, 3366, or Daiichi 2546, sizes 4 to 2/0.
Thread: White and red, size 3/0.
Tail: Grizzly saltwater neck hackle with pearl Krystal Flash.
Hackle collar: Grizzly.
Body: ½-inch-diameter pearl Corsair, EZ Body tubing, or Flexo tubing.

JACK GARTSIDE WAS A TERRIFIC FLY DESIGNER. HIS PATTERNS were usually very simple; using only a couple of materials, Jack could create a fly that would catch fish. Check out his other fly called the Gurgler in this book. Even a novice tier can fill a box full of his original patterns and be confident that he would have effective flies for his next fishing trip.

Mike Hogue, the proprietor of Badger Creek Fly Tying, an online fly-tying catalog, recently reminded me of Gartside's unique brand of creativity. Mike sent three flies Jack developed called the FishHead. Jack made the head of the original FishHead using a tough, flexible tubing he called Corsair. Today, most fly shops carry a product called EZ Body tubing, which is very similar to the original Corsair; these products are interchangeable.

To make the head of the fly, simply tie the end of a piece of EZ Body tubing behind the hook eye and facing forward; the tubing completely encircles the eye. Tie off and clip the thread. Next, push the tubing back toward the rear of the hook to form the head. Restart the thread on the tubing behind the hook eye. Pull the thread tight to form a bullet-shaped head, clip the excess tubing around the eye, and wrap the thread head.

Corsair is a bulletproof type of tubing. The FishHead is suitable for using wherever you find small baitfish. Change the colors of the materials to match the baitfish in your local waters, and be sure to tie a few FishHeads in black and bright attractor color schemes.

Coyote

Hook: Tiemco TMC811S, size 1.
Thread: Clear monofilament.
Eyes: Meadium Real Eyes with adhesive eyes on the sides.
Body: Flat pearl braided tinsel.
Monofilament spike: 40-pound-test monofilament.
Tail: Rabbit Zonker strip.
Wing: Bucktail.
Flash: Pearl Krystal Flash.
Spinner blade: Size #00 gold or nickel Colorado blade, a size #12 barrel swivel, and size #0 split ring.

A FLY-FISHING PAL CREATED THIS UNUSUAL PATTERN called the Coyote. A small spinner blade, tied to the underside of the hook, is the outstanding feature of this pattern.

I know some fly fishers might look askance at the Coyote because of the spinner blade, but then patterns tied using synthetic materials were once not considered proper "flies." It didn't take long, however, before anglers saw the value in Surf Candies and this whole host of new fly designs. Today these patterns are the staples of many fly boxes; in the world of saltwater fly fishing, using synthetic materials might even be more popular than natural ingredients.

There might not be a great difference between using a spinner blade and a rattle when tying a fly. These components are not traditional materials, yet both are designed to make noise and grab the attention of the fish. So why use one and not the other?

Casting the Coyote is easy. Even though it has a spinner blade, the blade rarely tangles in the leader.

The Coyote is a fine striped bass and bluefish fly, and it also catches its share of snook. It's an unusual pattern, but fun to tie and fish.

Half and Half

Hook: Mustad 34007, sizes 2 to 2/0.
Thread: Danville Flymaster Plus.
Eyes: Lead or chrome dumbbell.
Tail: Saddle hackles and Flashabou.
Collar: Bucktail.
Belly and back: Bucktail.

THE HALF AND HALF IS A BLEND OF TWO OF OUR BEST-known patterns: the Lefty's Deceiver and Clouser Minnow.

Look closely and you'll see features of the two flies. The hackle tail and bucktail belly and back are inspired by the Deceiver; the dumbbell eyes, tied on top of the shank so the hook flips over when fishing, are taken from the Clouser Minnow.

Even a novice tier can craft a fish-catching Half and Half. All fly shops carry the ingredients, and they are easy to tie to the hook. Let's start with the tail.

The length of the hackle tail is about one and one-half times the overall length of the hook. Strip the fluffy fibers from the base of the feathers until they are the correct length. Add a few strands of Flashabou or another brand of flash material on both sides of the hackle tail.

Tie the collar around the base of the tail. Do not use the bucktail fibers from the base of the tail. These are coarse and will flair like deer body hair. Clip the hair from the top two-thirds of the deer tail.

Tie the dumbbell eyes on top of the hook shank, but leave ample room to tie on the belly and back, and to wrap a neat thread head.

Tie the Half and Half in a range of colors. Red and white are classic colors for flies and lures, but an all-white, black, or chartreuse Half and Half also catches fish. You can also use these same materials to tie simple Deceivers and Clouser Minnows.

Tarpon Toy

Hook: Tiemco TMC811S or your favorite saltwater hook, size 3/0.
Thread: Brown Monocord for tying the tail, and switch to orange 3/0 for wrapping the nose of the fly.
Tail: Red squirrel tail hair, gold Flashabou, and furnace hackles.
Collar: Natural gray rabbit strip.
Eyes: Small yellow adhesive eyes.

THE TARPON TOY LOOKS GREAT WHEN STRIPPED THROUGH the water. The rabbit fur collar comes alive and gives the fly a lifelike swimming action.

There are two types of rabbit strips; the material you purchase should match the application for the flies you are tying. The most common are Zonker strips. These are cut with the fur flowing the same direction as the leather strips. They are perfect for making the tails on flies.

The second are crosscut rabbit strips. This material is cut across the hide of the rabbit so the fur flows perpendicular to the direction of the strips. Select crosscut rabbit strips for wrapping around the hook, such as tying the collar of the Tarpon Toy.

The Tarpon Toy is one of Captain Lenny Moffo's patterns. Captain Moffo is a topnotch guide working the waters of the Florida Keys. I met Lenny many years ago while tying flies at the Miami Boat Show. Lenny came up from the Keys for the day, and it was great learning more about fishing the Keys from such an accomplished angler. As you can see, he is also an expert fly tier. His patterns go through hundreds of hours of testing and tweaking; if Captain Moffo says it's a good pattern, it is probably something you should add to your personal fly box.

Snag-Free Delight

Hook: Plastic worm hook, sizes 2 to 3/0.
Thread: Clear monofilament.
Body: Pearl Mylar tubing.
Belly: Pink SF Flash Blend.
Back: White, yellow, and chartreuse SF Flash Blend.
Topping: Peacock herl.
Eyes: Large 3-D eyes.

CAPTAIN CHRIS NEWSOME SPECIALIZES IN FISHING VIRGINIA'S Chesapeake Bay. If you haven't visited this area, you should: it is rich in gamefish and fly-fishing opportunities.

Captain Newsome fishes the entire Hampton Roads area including the waters surrounding the Chesapeake Bay Tunnel Bridge. If you hit it right, the water flowing under the bridge can contain hundreds of striped bass, and you can actually become weary from catching them. I once fished this area at about 3 o'clock in the morning. Bass were boiling on the surface of the out-going tide, and we hooked a fish on almost every cast. Amazing!

In addition to being an expert angler, Captain Newsome is an inventive fly designer. In this case, when tying his Snag-Free Delight, he uses a hook designed for fishing conventional plastic worms. The hook is bent behind the eye, which encourages the fly to ride with the point on top. Chris first wraps lead wire on the shank to ensure that the pattern rides in the correct position. You can fish the Snag-Free Delight around pilings and near the bottom with little fear of hooking nothing but the fish. Plastic-worm hooks also have large gaps that aid in hooking fish.

This Snag-Free Delight is tied using only synthetic materials, but Captain Newsome makes larger versions using a blend of hackles and synthetic hairs for the wings. Tie the Snag-Free Delight in sizes and colors to match real baitfish, and make a few in attractor colors such as chartreuse, orange, and black.

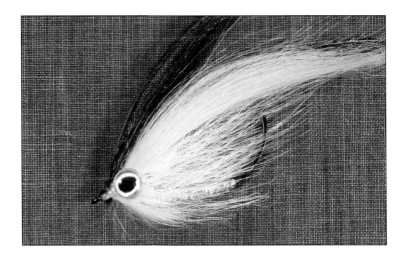

Inside Counts

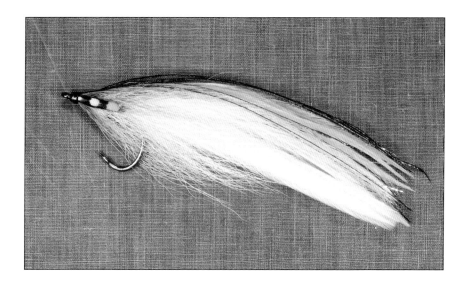

Hook: Tiemco TMC811S or your favorite saltwater hook, size 3/0.
Thread: Black 3/0.
Weight: Plastic-worm cone weight.
Belly: Chartreuse and olive bucktail.
Flanks: Pink and white bucktail.
Wing: White and light olive hackles, and pearl Flashabou.
Back: Chartreuse and olive bucktail.
Topping: Peacock herl.
Cheeks: Jungle cock.

WHEN I OPENED CAPTAIN CHRIS NEWSOME'S PACKAGE AND examined his flies, I thought that Inside Counts was an odd name for a pattern. The "inside" of what? *It's probably someplace where he fishes,* I thought. He is a top guide fishing Virginia's Chesapeake Bay, so I assumed this was a fly he used up inside the Bay.

I was wrong.

The Inside Counts is one of the most beautiful patterns in this book. The jungle cock cheeks and peacock herl topping gives it a classic look. But, the blend of bucktail and saddle hackles give it a very fishy appearance; when retrieved through the water, the colors flow together and make the fly look like a baitfish.

But, it is what's inside the fly that counts.

Captain Newsome slips a small plastic-worm cone weight onto the hook before tying the fly. This adds heft to the pattern and acts as a spreader; any materials tied on behind the hook eye splay around the cone. Chris ties on the hackles and pink bucktail behind the cone, and he places the belly and back in front of the cone. That's a great idea!

I experimented with some hooks and lead cones. Although the lead is soft, getting the cone into position is not easy. You may have to widen the hole in the cones using a drill, and gripping it with pliers will help. But, the extra effort pays off; this is an ingenious idea that you can use to tie interesting weighted flies.

Stinger Deep Minnow

Hooks: Two regular saltwater hooks, size 2.
Thread: Olive 3/0.
Eyes: Medium chrome dumbbell.
Connecting wire: 50-pound-test steel leader.
Tail: White calftail or another fine-fibered hair, and strands of pearl Krystal Flash or a similar material.
Body: Pearl braided tinsel.
Wing: Pink and olive bucktail.

HERE IS A GREAT TAKE ON THE VENERABLE CLOUSER DEEP Minnow.

The Clouser Minnow is one of the bestselling patterns of all time. It is also one of the first patterns taught in beginning fly-tying classes. Why? Because it catches fish!

But what if the fish have sharp teeth? Bluefish, for example, are tough on flies. Not only do they destroy patterns, their teeth easily slice through monofilament and fluorocarbon leaders. In the flash of an eye, you can go from a solid hookup to a limp line. This is very frustrating.

The Stinger Deep Minnow solves both of these problems. A stinger hook, linked to the main body hook using a piece of stout wire leader, keeps the pattern well forward when hooking a fish. This protects both the fly and leader from the teeth of the fish. It's a simple solution to these common problems, and you can use this design on most flies.

The added advantage is that you can use a standard leader, rather than a stiff wire bite tippet, when targeting bluefish.

Use a loop knot when tying any type of Clouser Minnow to your leader. The loop knot remains slightly open, not cinched tight against the hook eye, so the pattern moves freely at the end of the leader. This allows the Clouser Minnow and similarly weighted flies to bob up and down when retrieved through the water, giving the fly an added realistic swimming action.

Dinah-Moe Drum

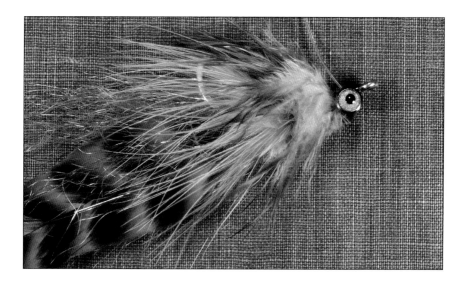

Hook: Regular saltwater hook, size 3/0.
Thread: Olive 3/0.
Eyes: Large chrome dumbbell with adhesive eyes.
Tail: Grizzly hackles dyed golden olive.
Collar: Copper Angel Hair, golden-yellow marabou, and grizzly marabou dyed gold.
Weed guard: 20-pound-test stiff monofilament.

S.S. FLIES IS A UNIQUE FLY-TYING OUTFIT BASED IN MY HOME state of Maine. Every year the guys at S.S. Flies pump out more than 20,000 flies—all tied in their establishment—for guides and fly shops around the world. That's an amazing output!

In addition to making many standard patterns, they also design custom flies to meet the demands of the most accomplished saltwater guides and anglers. Their custom pattern called the Dinah-Moe Drum is a good example of their creativity.

According to Peter Smith, the head man at S.S. Flies, "For the longest time we knew we needed a big, heavy redfish fly. The pattern called Willy the Pimp is big and effective but isn't terribly heavy, and our Clousers are heavy but not really big. Finally, we came up with this fly called the Dinah-Moe Drum. It's four inches long and heavy enough to get down to the fish quickly."

Some anglers search for trophy-size redfish. They require large patterns to catch these big fish. Dinah-Moe Drum is a good answer to this problem.

This is the golden-olive Dinah-Moe Drum, but S.S. Flies also ties it in chartreuse and natural-colored materials. The Angel Hair and marabou give the fly excellent swimming action in the water. This fly would also be a top candidate for catching striped bass and many other species of our favorite gamefish.

Boehm's Gurgler

Hook: Long-shank saltwater hook, size 2/0.
Thread: Tan 3/0.
Tail: Tan rabbit Zonker strip and tan craft fur.
Body: Pearl Krystal Flash.
Collar: A large tuft of tan rabbit fur.
Back: Tan closed-cell foam.

ACCORDING TO PETER SMITH OF S. S. FLIES, "WE DEVELOPED this Gurgler years ago for Capt. Alex Boehm. He had just signed on as a full-time private guide for an angler in Key West, a man who had the means to employ a captain on his personal staff. One of Alex's first big trips was to Ascension Bay and he needed a baby tarpon fly. This was before we had the ability to send photos back and forth, so we talked about a few patterns and I started tying samples and sending them back and forth; it took a while. We ended up with a Gurgler-style fly with a rabbit fur tail and front collar. Alex wanted a fly that would keep pulsing after being stripped, and fish in or just under the surface."

Yes, tarpon do take surface flies; this is how I have caught many baby tarpon. It's a fun game, especially when fishing canals under street and porch lights. You see a swirl and hear a watery smack several feet beyond the end of your line, and you set the hook. Sometimes the line goes tight and you feel a sharp thump, the sure sign that you are into a fish.

Tie this pattern for catching tarpon, but it will attract any other species of fish that will suck in floating flies.

CHAPTER TWO

Match the Hatch Saltwater Style: Flies That Imitate Common Baitfish

King's Hoo Fly
(Anchovy)

Hook: Gamakatsu SL12S, size 2.
Thread: Fine Uni-Mono.
Tail: Tan craft fur.
Body and head: Dark tan and yellow over silver minnow belly and pink Senyo's Laser Dub, coated and shaped with Liquid Fusion.
Eyes: Fish-Skull Living Eyes.

JONNY KING STARTED TYING SALTWATER FLIES IN 1990. HE
has fly fished throughout much of the world and has caught almost every
species of inshore saltwater fish. Jonny especially enjoys fishing for striped
bass and bluefish on Cape Cod Bay and New York Harbor. When he's not
fishing, you might find Jonny playing jazz at one of Manhattan's music
hotspots.

Jonny taught himself to tie as a young teenager reading Poul Jorgenson's
instructional books, and has tied virtually every kind of pattern: tiny dry
flies, bass bugs, steelhead patterns, Northeast striper flies, tuna flies, and flats
patterns for bonefish, tarpon, permit, and snook. He has come a very long
way since reading Poul's books, and now creates his flies using a blend of
natural and synthetic ingredients. This anchovy version of his Hoo Fly is a
little unusual in that he tied it using only durable synthetic materials.

Senyo's Laser Dub is a product of Hareline Dubbin. Hareline Dubbin
teamed with pattern designer Greg Senyo to create this useful blend of Ice
Dub and acrylic fibers. You'll find Senyo's Laser Dub in many well-stocked
fly shops.

Liquid Fusion, which is used to form the head of the fly, is a clear ure-
thane adhesive that is nontoxic and has very little order. Look for Liquid
Fusion in your local craft store.

King's Kinky Muddler
(Sand Eel)

Hook: Gamakatsu SL12S, size 2/0.
Thread: Uni-Mono.
Tail: Light purple bucktail under pairs of olive and rusty brown saddle hackles tied tented so they create an inverted V.
Body and head: Brown over white Slinky Fiber or Slinky Fiber Flash Blend.
Eyes: Fish-Skull Living Eyes.

HERE IS JONNY KING'S INTERPRETATION OF A SAND EEL, and it's a real winner! This pattern is easy to make and it will fill an important slot in your fly box.

We typically think of finding sand eels on Northeast fishing flats, but they are far more widespread. You will find sand eels along the coasts of Europe from Spain to Scotland, and in the Mediterranean.

The term "sand eel" is used to describe a large number of species of long, narrow fish; they really aren't eels. They prefer habitat with soft, sandy bottoms. Sand eels burrow into the bottom in order to escape predators, including many species of our favorite gamefish.

Most sand eel imitations are tied from three to about six inches long. Select soft materials that give your flies a flowing, swimming action when stripped through the water. And, although there is a temptation to fish these patterns slowly, real sand eels can move quickly through the water when frightened. Use an erratic retrieve when fishing a sand eel imitation, giving your fly a natural darting action.

Fish-Skull Living Eyes, which Jonny King uses on this pattern, is a product of Flymen Fishing Company. These eyes are very realistic looking and make the head of the fly really "pop" to attract the attention of fish.

King's Kinky Muddler (Atlantic Herring)

Hook: Owner 5320 Spinner bait hook, size 5/0.
Thread: Fine Uni-Mono.
Tail: White bucktail under pairs of pink, pale green and blue hackles tied tented so they create an inverted V.
Body: Two collars of light blue bucktail, and a collar of pink and blue marabou wrapped on the hook.
Head: Blue over white Slinky Fiber or Slinky Fiber Flash Blend, V-tied and trimmed, with pink cheeks.
Eyes: Fish-Skull Living Eyes.

FLY DESIGNER JONNY KING TIES HIS SERIES OF KINKY MUD-
dler patterns using half natural and half synthetic materials. The tails are
tented saddle hackles, and the heads are Kinky Fiber Flash Blend clipped
and trimmed like deer hair. A Kinky Muddler has a dense head that looks
opaque like the head of a baitfish, and the sparse tail flutters like the tail of a
real fish. King says, "The purpose of tenting the saddles is to create a fuller,
rounder body profile and to maximize movement."

Here we see Jonny's imitation of an Atlantic herring. Use this pattern
wherever herring play an important part of the forage base for gamefish.

Slinky Fiber is sometimes packaged under the name Slinky Fibre; they
are the same materials. Slinky Fiber is a product of an innovative company
called H2O. Slinky Fiber is a kinky, fine synthetic fiber that is great for
tying bulky flies without having to pile on a bunch of material, or you can
use only a pinch of material to tie a slender pattern. Slinky Fiber comes in
twenty colors and is very easy to use. Change colors of materials to make
imitations of mackerel, mullet, and generic amber-looking baitfish. If your
local fly shop doesn't stock Slinky Fiber, you may substitute with FisHair or
a similar synthetic material.

Farrar's Peanut Bunker
MV Baitfish

Hook: Mustad C68SZ, size 5/0.
Thread: Danville Clear Monofilament.
Wing: Bronzeback and peacock Slinky Fiber Flash Blend, over olive and bronzeback, over yellow.
Underbelly: Off-white Slinky Fiber Flash Blend.
Throat: Electric pink Angel Hair.
Eyes: Epoxy 3-D.
Adhesive: Plasti Dip.

IF YOU SPEND ANY TIME FLY FISHING ON THE EAST COAST, you will hear the term "peanut bunker." A bunker, sometimes called a pogie or mossbunker, is a menhaden. It is one of the most common and important baitfish on the coast. Once ranging from Nova Scotia to Florida, their range has been diminished, but not their importance to high-quality fishing. In fact, the health of striped bass and bluefish populations is often directly related to the health of the menhaden population. A peanut bunker is a small, juvenile menhaden. (Curiously, I have never heard anyone refer to a "peanut pogie," which actually sounds a little poetic.)

Anyway, late summer and into the fall, striped bass will key into juvenile menhaden. These small baitfish are typically two to three inches long, and you should use a pattern of matching size. There are dozens of imitations of peanut bunker, and Steve Farrar's Peanut Bunker MV Baitfish is one of the best. It is just the right size and shape, has the perfect amount of flash, and those eyes convince predator fish that it is something good to eat. Even though this is a small pattern, few striped bass and bluefish will escape the large size 5/0 hook.

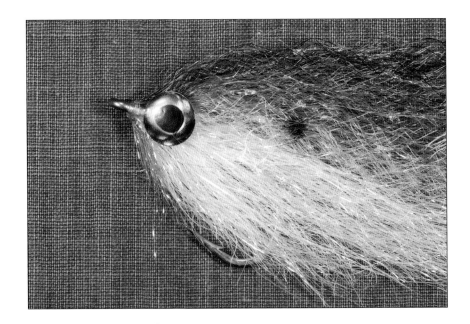

Farrar's Anchovy MV Baitfish

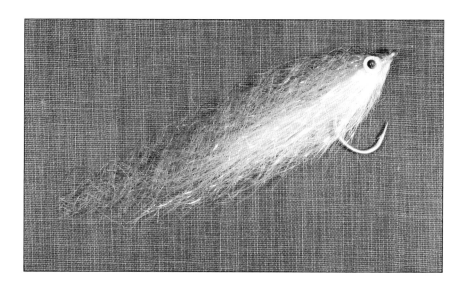

Hook: Varivas 990S, size 1/0.
Thread: Clear monofilament.
Wing: Brown, olive, and sea blue over anchovy Slinky Fiber Flash Blend.
Underbelly: White UV Slinky Fiber Flash Blend.
Flash: Pearl/green and pearl/blue Angel Hair.
Eyes: Epoxy 3-D.
Adhesive: Plasti Dip.

I DID SOME RESEARCH ABOUT ANCHOVIES, AND DISCOVERED some interested facts on the website of the National Oceanic and Atmospheric Administration. When you consider these facts, there is little wonder that anchovies are an important source of food for our West Coast fisheries.

There are more than twenty species of anchovies in the family Engraulidae. The northern anchovy, *Engraulis mordax*, is commercially harvested off the West Coast, mainly as bait for catching other fish although it is sometimes processed as fishmeal. Once upon a time, when the Pacific sardine fishery collapsed, anchovies were caught and sold for human consumption. Although the terms sardine and anchovy are sometimes used interchangeably, make no mistake: they are not the same fish. Also, according to the NOAA website, anchovies along the Pacific Coast are not being overfished, which is a true marvel considering the long list of depleted fish stocks.

An anchovy grows five to eight inches in length, so you should tie imitations in similar sizes. Even though anchovies are found in the Pacific Ocean and parts of Europe, Farrar's Anchovy MV Baitfish is a pattern that has wide application. Use this fly wherever small baitfish are on the gamefish menu. It would be particularly effective for matching many forms of similar-sized bait along the East Coast of the United States.

5-Minute Finger Mullet

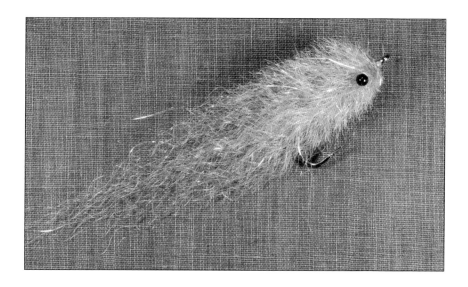

Hook: Daiichi 2546, size 2 or 1.
Thread: Monofilament.
Wing: Steve Farrar's Flash Blend—shrimp, gray, and mullet brown.
Eyes: Large black EP Crab/Shrimp Eyes.
Head: Steve Farrar's Flash Blend—dubbing brush gray and mullet brown.

LET'S TALK ABOUT THE MULLET, NOT THE GOOFY HAIR style but the fish.

Mullet are very widespread around the world and so are an important source of food for many of our favorite gamefish. A mullet has two dorsal fins, a small mouth, and no distinguishable lateral line. Mullet are sometimes called jumping or happy mullet because they occasionally leap out of the water and skip along the surface. Mullet will also gather in large schools.

Mullet are generally small, and real finger mullets are very popular with bait fishermen. Fly imitations of mullet are excellent for catching striped bass and bluefish along the New Jersey Coast and nearby waters. Mullets are also common in Florida, so have a few imitations in your fly box when fishing in the Sunshine State.

Drew Chicone uses a Steve Farrar Dubbing Brush for fashioning the head of his 5-Minute Finger Mullet. A dubbing brush is a piece of thin doubled wire similar to an extra-large piece of chenille. The dubbing brush can contain many types of fur as well as natural and synthetic hair. In this case, the brush contains Steve Farrar's Flash Blend.

After making the long fur wing of the fly, tie the end of the dubbing brush to the hook at the base of the wing. Wrap the brush up the hook shank; brush back the fibers after each wrap to prevent trapping the fur. Next, tie and cut off the remaining piece of brush (save it for tying another fly), and clip the head to shape. Dubbing brushes are easy and quick to use, and you will be satisfied with the results.

GT Pinfish

Hook: Daiichi 2546, sizes 4 and 2.
Thread: Clear monofilament.
Tail: Tan craft fur and lavender DNA Holo-Fusion.
Belly: White saltwater yak hair and blue/pearl Angel Hair.
Back: Tan saltwater yak hair and gold Angel Hair.
Eyes: 8-millimeter gold Orvis Jurassic Eyes.
Gills: Red saltwater yak hair.

A PINFISH IS A SMALL BAITFISH THAT GROWS TO LITTLE more than four inches long. Pinfish exist from the Mexican Gulf Coast and Bermuda along the Atlantic Coast of the United States all the way to Massachusetts. Although adult pinfish prefer deeper waters, you'll encounter immature pinfish around mangroves, pilings, and jetties. As a result, tie smaller versions of this pattern to closely match the local bait. Sea trout, red drum, and lady fish are especially fond of pinfish.

Yak hair is a particularly good fly-tying material. The fibers are long and soft, and have a great flowing action when drawn through the water. It is ideal for tying the bodies on baitfish imitations. If your local fly shop doesn't stock yak hair, you can usually substitute with craft fur.

Yak hair actually comes from yaks, which are ox-like animals native to the Himalayas and Tibet. Curiously, large quantities of yak were imported for the manufacture of wigs and hair extensions, but it was discovered that many people are allergic to the fibers when worn for prolonged periods of time. Fortunately, yak hair is still being imported so we can use it to tie fish-catching flies. Use it as the main component in a body or add some craft fur or bucktail. Also include a few strands of Krystal Flash to add sparkle to your fly.

Kintz's Major Herring

Hook: Regular saltwater hook, size 3/0.
Thread: White 3/0.
Tail: White saddle hackles with bright blue Polar Fiber on top and gray Polar Fiber on the bottom. Pearl Flashabou on the sides.
Body: Mylar braid.
Flanks: Pearl Flashabou.
Underwing: Gray bucktail.
Wing: Blue and black Polar Fiber, and pearl Flashabou.
Belly: Gray bucktail.
Eyes: Gold 3D eyes.

THOMAS KINTZ CREATED THIS PATTERN HE CALLS THE Major Herring for Umpqua Feather Merchants. It's a terrific option for when striped bass, bluefish, and other gamefish are feeding on herring.

The trouble with tying a tall, full-bodied fly such as the Major Herring is creating a fly that loses its profile when fishing. On an ill-conceived pattern, the soft feathers and furs collapse around the hook when the fly is drawn through the water. A simple solution is to tie a few strands of bucktail to the top of the fly as an underwing, and then place other material—in this case Polar Fiber—on top. The bucktail holds the wing up, maintaining the tall silhouette of a real herring.

I have fished for striped bass that were busting in schools of herring. When they are keying into this bait, the fish easily mistake a well-made fly for the real bait. I typically fish a pattern such as Kintz's Major Herring using a line with a sinking tip. Since the fish are feeding aggressively, they are not leader shy; a 15-pound-test tippet will not dissuade the bass from striking. Since you are using a sinking line, the leader only needs to be four to five feet in length.

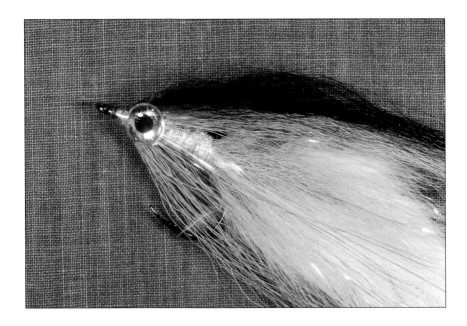

Big Eye Baitfish
Mackerel

Hook: Regular saltwater hook, size 1.
Thread: Black 2/0.
Tail: White saddle hackle and green grizzly saddle hackle.
Back: Pearl, green, and black crinkled Flashabou or a similar material, and black bucktail.
Belly: White bucktail.
Throat: Red pearl Krystal Flash.
Cheeks: Green holographic sheet material.
Eyes: Silver adhesive eyes.

PAGE ROGERS HAS HAD A LASTING IMPACT ON SALTWATER fly fishing. She has spent many seasons designing patterns and sharing what she knows with fellow tiers. Although she is well into retirement years, I saw Page at a recent fly-fishing show. She looked fit and still ready to tangle with a strong striped bass. Check the bins at your local fly shop, and you will find her patterns the Slim Jim, Rogers Sand Eel, and this Big Eye Baitfish Mackerel.

Mackerel are a common baitfish, and there are many patterns designed to match them. The challenge is to re-create the marble-like green turquoise and pearl color of the back of the fish. Page uses a blend of the feathers—white and green grizzly—and flash material to imitate the back and sides of a mackerel.

The foil cheeks give the head of the fly a solid appearance, and of course a place to position the adhesive eyes. Coat the eyes with a drop of adhesive to lock them to the foil.

Use the Big Eye Baitfish Mackerel along the Atlantic Coast wherever you might encounter schools of mackerel. They are a favorite prey of striped bass and bluefish. Page uses this design to tie the Big Eye Herring, and also flies in the basic fish-catching colors black, blue, and chartreuse. Simply select materials in your favorite colors.

Cowen's Albie Anchovy

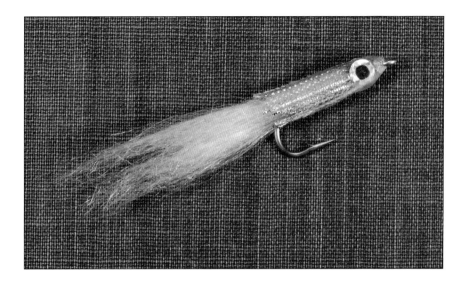

Hook: Tiemco 811S, size 4.
Thread: Fine Danville Clear Monofilament.
Wing: Shrimp Polar Fibre.
Underbelly: Shrimp Polar Fibre.
Belly sac: Silver Gliss N Glow.
Body: Medium natural EZ Body.
Eyes: Silver prismatic adhesive eyes.
Adhesive: Clear Cure Goo or a similar light-activated adhesive.

HENRY COWEN IS A MASTER FLY DESIGNER. AFTER SPENDING most of his life in the Northeast chasing striped bass and bluefish, he now lives in North Carolina and plies his flies in those waters. He is also an authority at catching freshwater striped bass.

Many of the flies in this book are tied using Tuffleye, Clear Cure Goo, or one of the other light-activated adhesive products; you'll see those materials listed in the pattern recipes. These adhesives are taking the place of epoxy on many tying benches. These acrylic products are cured using a blue or ultraviolet light; because of safety concerns, the distributors recommend using a blue light.

Acrylic adhesives come in convenient syringes. Unlike epoxy, they require no mixing, they don't cure until you apply the blue light, and there is no waste. To cure the adhesive, apply the material to the fly, and then shine the light; the adhesive fully cures in twenty to thirty seconds.

There is a small initial investment when working with light-cured acrylics, primarily for the flashlight blue light; all the distributors sell kits containing lights and adhesives. After purchasing the light and using the adhesive in the kit, you'll only need to purchase additional syringes of adhesive to tie more flies. The convenience of using this extremely durable material, and the fact that there is no waste, makes it a very strong competitor to epoxy.

Cowen's Sand Eel

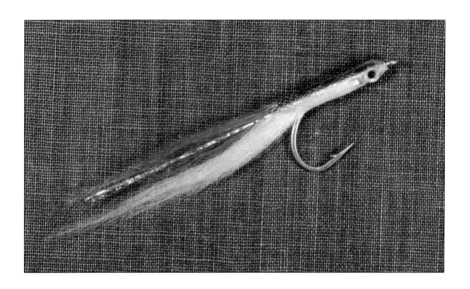

Hook: Gamakatsu SC15, size 1/0.
Thread: Danville Clear Monofilament.
Wing: Olive and white Polar Fibre.
Lateral line: Narrow holographic tinsel.
Body: Small natural EZ Body.
Eyes: Silver prismatic adhesive eyes.
Head: Clear Cure Goo.

LET ME TELL YOU A TRUE STORY ABOUT THE IMPORTANCE
of sand eels to good fishing.

Many years ago, my family was visiting West Dennis Beach at the mouth
of the Bass River on Cape Cod. Due to tide conditions, fishing was best
early in the morning and early evening. This schedule allowed ample time
during the day to tour the Cape with the family.

One hot afternoon, we stopped at Dennis Beach for a swim. It was low
tide and the sun was bright in a cloudless sky. Fishing seemed out of the
question, but then a funny thing happened.

Boats started gathering at the edge of the sand flats; the water was little more than a couple of feet deep. The occupants of the boats had rakes
with long handles, and they began raking the sand. A couple of automobiles
pulled into the parking lot, and the occupants got out and headed into the
shallow water with rakes and buckets, and also started raking the sand. They
were all collecting sand eels. It wasn't long before swarms of gulls gathered
and started feeding on the eels. It was a sight to see!

Some time passed and another automobile pulled into the parking lot.
Two fellows got out of the car and strung up fly rods. They watched the
bait collectors and birds for a few minutes, and then waded into the middle
of the action. Both anglers made single casts and were fast into fish. Despite
the low water and blazing sun—typically very poor fishing conditions—the
eels attracted a large school of striped bass. I immediately retrieved my rod
from our car, waded into the skinny water on the flats, and was quickly into
a bass. It was a fine day of terrific fishing that I will never forget.

Mayan Cichlid

Hook: Gamakatsu SC-15, size 2/0.
Thread: Monofilament.
Belly: A blend of white and tan saltwater yak hair, and a blend of white and orange saltwater yak hair.
Back: A blend of olive, chartreuse, and tan saltwater yak hair, and a blend of olive and brown saltwater yak hair.
Throat: Orange saltwater yak hair.
Eyes: 8-millimeter orange or yellow doll eyes.

CICHLIDS ARE PART OF THE FAMILY OF FISH CALLED CICHLIDAE. This family contains more than 1,600 species, and more are still being discovered. Typically found in fresh water, some species do live in near-shore brackish water and are available as food to some of our favorite gamefish. Some cichlids display a rainbow of colors and are quite beautiful; they have long been popular among aquarium hobbyists.

The Mayan cichlid is a native to South America, and is now found in the waters surrounding South Florida. Most biologists agree that Mayan cichlids, which are considered an invasive species in the Northern Hemisphere, were introduced to Florida by people discarding unwanted fish from their aquariums and perhaps fish farm escapees. Today you'll find these fish in South Florida's brackish creeks and canals. They are a good source of food for tarpon and snook.

This pattern calls for a large number of colors of yak hair. While this is fine tying material, your local fly shop might not have all of these colors. The goal is to create a fly with a tall, narrow profile; kinky-fibered yak hair creates bulk on the hook without using too much material. Ordinary craft fur is a poor substitute because the fibers will collapse around the hook when the fly becomes wet and you'll lose the necessary profile. If you must substitute with another ingredient, try synthetic FisHair or a similar kinky material.

ALF Stir Fry

Hook: Long-shank saltwater hook, size 3/0.
Thread: Clear monofilament.
Belly: White Ultra Hair.
Flanks: Chartreuse or yellow Ultra Hair and pearl Flashabou.
Back: Peacock Krystal Flash and green Flashabou.
Side of head: Red Super Hair.
Under the head: Copper narrow Flashabou.

KATE AND BILL HOWE ARE TWO PROFESSIONAL FLY FISHERS and pattern designers from California. They have created many terrific off-shore patterns tied on monster double-hook rigs to smaller patterns such as the ALF Stir Fry.

According to Trey Combs, in his book *Bluewater Fly Fishing*, ALF is an acronym for "Any Little Fellow." The ALF Stir Fry is the Howes' imitation of an anchovy, but you can use the design to mimic many of the baitfish in your local waters. Change colors of materials to match these baits.

This is a commercially tied version of the ALF Stir Fry. Although it is a fine looking fly, in *Bluewater Fly Fishing* the Howes give detailed instructions on how they blend colors of materials to create convincing looking bait-fish imitations. They also blend Super Hair, Ultra Hair, and an ingredient called Ocean Hair when tying the wing, taking advantage of the properties offered by all of these materials. Check your local well-stocked fly shop for these materials, and ask the clerk about substitutes. Many synthetic ingredi-ents are packaged under different trade names, and you will discover other materials for tying similar flies.

Many tiers prefer using synthetic materials because they make it easy to reproduce successful flies. The quality and colors of natural ingredients can vary widely, so it is sometimes difficult to purchase more materials to tie those winning patterns. With synthetic materials, the quality and colors are almost always identical, so you can easily restock your bench and keep tying.

Skok's Mushmouth

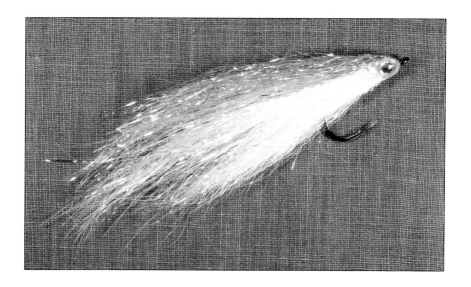

Hook: Owner AKI 2/0 or other short shank-hook, size 2.
Thread: Monofilament.
Tail: White Super Hair and gold Flashabou.
Belly: Pearl Wing 'N Flash.
Back: Peacock Light Brite.

DAVID SKOK IS A LEADING OUTDOORS PHOTOGRAPHER based in Boston. Although he lives in the Northeast, David travels the world in search of good fishing and photographs. You'll find his great photos in most of the leading fly-fishing magazines, and it has been featured in several beautiful books.

David is also an inventive fly designer. His Mushmouth series of baitfish patterns are some of his most famous flies. They are tied using entirely synthetic materials so they are very easy to reproduce.

After starting the thread on the hook, tie the first bunch of Super Hair or your favorite fine-fibered synthetic hair material; craft fur, however, won't work for the Mushmouth. Study the picture of the fly and look for something to match. Coat the material right behind the hook with Softex or a similar clear, fast-drying finish. This stiffens the fibers and helps the fly maintain its shape when fishing. Continue adding small bunches of material to form the belly and back of the fly.

To complete the Mushmouth, pinch the front of the fly between your fingers to flatten the head. Place an eye on each side of the head. Coat the head and eyes with a generous drop of Softex.

The Mushmouth is a flashy fly that stands out in a large school of baitfish. It is also extremely durable. Select colors of materials to tie Mushmouths to match many of the baitfish in your favorite water.

Surf Candies

Hook: Regular saltwater hook, sizes 6 to 2.
Thread: Clear monofilament.
Tail: Ultra Hair or bucktail, and thin Flashabou or Krystal Flash.
Body: Silver or pearl tinsel.
Head: Epoxy or light–activated acrylic.

THIRTY YEARS AGO, THERE WAS A FLY SHOP IN KNOXVILLE, Tennessee, called The Creel. One Saturday while visiting the shop, four or five fellows were crowded around the tying table, making a new type of fly. It was something featured in the latest issue of what was then called *American Angler & Fly Tyer* magazine. They were having fun making the pattern, but debated whether it was really a fly; the synthetic fiber tail and epoxy head broke all conventions about what a fly should look like. There was no question, however, that the fly certainly looked fishy.

I didn't know it at the time, but I was looking at Surf Candies, the revolutionary flies developed by Bob Popovics.

More than two decades later, while interviewing Bob about the history of Surf Candies, he explained that he developed his idea in the 1970s. He needed flies that toothy bluefish couldn't destroy. The first Surf Candies were nothing more than bucktail streamers with epoxy heads. Eventually, Bob made the tails using FisHair and similar synthetic fibers, and he added eyes to his flies. Using these materials, he designed Surf Candies in colors and sizes to imitate spearing, small sand eels, and a wide variety of the baitfish he found in his home waters along the New Jersey shore.

Here we see the most recent generation of Surf Candies. The heads are flanked with small pieces of foil called Fleye Foils, and rather than using epoxy, Bob coated the heads with a light-activated acrylic called Tuffleye.

The Surf Candy is a very adaptable pattern. Add a small metal cone to the nose before tying the fly to create the Deep Candy. If you fish tropical waters, use the Surf Candy design to tie an imitation of a needlefish that no barracuda can destroy. The Surf Candy is bulletproof.

Thunder Creek Bunker

Hook: Long-shank saltwater hook, size 1.
Thread: White 6/0.
Body: Gray and olive bucktail for the back, pale yellow bucktail for the belly, and a few strands of silver Krystal Flash.
Gills: Red enamel paint.
Eyes: White and black enamel paint.

IN THE EARLY 1970S, NEW YORK'S KEITH FULSHER PUBLISHED *Tying and Fishing the Thunder Creek Series*. In this small book, he described how to make a family of patterns he calls Thunder Creek streamers. In essence, Keith applied the idea of matching the hatch to making imitations of freshwater baitfish. His Thunder Creek flies match the shape, sizes, and colors of black-nosed dace, perch, immature trout, and more. His flies look fit and trim in the vise, and in the water they become sleek and streamlined. Until this point, most tiers made baitfish imitations using saddle hackles, marabou, or bucktail for the wings of flies; Keith used bucktail to make the heads as well as the bodies of his Thunder Creeks. (Keith's idea was not entirely new. Decades before, Carrie Stevens also made reverse-bucktail flies, but these were overshadowed by her famous feather-wing streamers such as the Gray Ghost.)

In 2006, I collaborated with Keith to write a new edition of his book, this time titled *Thunder Creek Flies: Tying and Fishing the Classic Baitfish Imitations*. In addition to featuring an expanded list of freshwater streamers, Keith included a series of wonderful imitations of saltwater baitfish. He used the same tying methods, but selected larger stainless steel hooks and bucktail in colors to match saltwater forage. These lightweight flies are easy to tie and cast, and assume the shape of baitfish when stripped through the water.

Here we see Keith's rendition of a baby bunker. This fly will become one of your favorite patterns if you fish for striped bass.

Thunder Creek Tinker Mackerel

Hook: Long-shank saltwater hook, size 1.
Thread: White 6/0.
Wing: Grizzly saddle hackle dyed light olive.
Body: Gray and dark blue bucktail for the back, white bucktail for the belly, and a few strands of silver Krystal Flash.
Gills: Red enamel paint.
Eyes: White and black enamel paint.

SMALL MACKEREL, OFTEN CALLED TINKER MACKEREL, ARE favorite forage for striped bass and bluefish. You'll want some type of tinker mackerel imitation in your fly box, and Keith Fulsher's Thunder Creek Tinker Mackerel is a great candidate.

Selecting the right materials when tying a Thunder Creek pattern is critical. The pegboard in the tying section of your local fly shop will be filled with packaged bucktails, but not all will work for making a nice Thunder Creek. Sort through the tails and reject those with crinkled or wavy hair; this hair will not make a sleek, streamlined fly. Look for tails that have long, straight hair in the desired colors.

When tying the fly, clip the hair from about the top two-thirds of the bucktail. The hair in the bottom one-third of the tail is thicker and behaves more like deer body hair when tying; tighten the thread, and this hair will flair.

Most tiers use entirely too much hair when tying Thunder Creeks. Tie a spare fly, and you will be happy with the results. And use only a few sprigs of Krystal Flash to add just a dash of flash to the fly.

Tie the bucktail to the top and bottom of the hook pointing forward over the eye. Fold the hair back and pinch the head of the fly. Make two or three firm thread wraps to form the body of the fly. Release the thread and check your work. If you are pleased with the appearance of the fly, you can whip-finish and clip the thread; if you think you can do better, unwrap the thread and try again.

Keith coats the heads of his flies with epoxy. Select thirty-minute epoxy so you can coat the heads of several flies at a time.

The Thunder Creek Tinker Mackerel has a wing of grizzly saddle hackles dyed light olive. This imitates the colored barring of a real mackerel.

Hines's Walking Cinder Worm

Hook: Regular saltwater hook, size 2.
Thread: Black 3/0.
Body: Red and brown chenille or Crystal Chenille, and red closed-cell foam.

REAL CINDER WORMS, WHICH RANGE ALONG THE ENTIRE East Coast, generally measure one to four inches long. They have black heads and pinkish red to brownish bodies. Cinder worms spend most of their lives burrowing in the mud bottoms of bays and estuaries until the time is right to emerge and spawn. At these times they swarm to the surface and mate. They are easy feed for gamefish and generate some of the most exciting fly fishing of the season for striped bass, tarpon, and more. Successful anglers have patterns that match real cinder worms; they enjoy saltwater fly-fishing's version of match the hatch.

The cinder worm emergence may begin in mid-April and last until the middle of June. Water temperatures are one of the keys: in the Northeast, ideal water temperatures range from the mid-50s to the mid-60s. Each emergence begins in the evening near the time of the full moon and increases to a maximum intensity during successive nights.

Cinder worm imitations are generally simple flies. Hines's Walking Cinder Worm, featuring a head and tail of buoyant closed-cell foam, floats on or right under the surface of the water. Cast the fly out, and use a very slow retrieve. The bright moon will illuminate the water, so keep your eye peeled for a large swirl in the water, a sure sign that a fish has taken your fly.

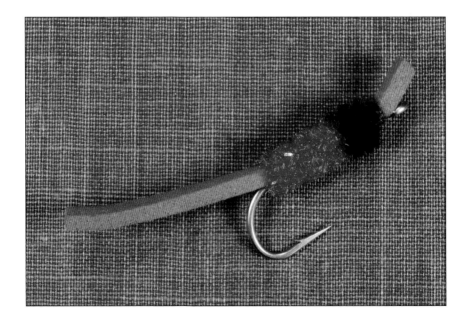

Hines's Simple Cinder Worm

Hook: Regular saltwater hook, size 2.
Thread: Black 3/0.
Tail: Red marabou.
Body: Red and brown chenille or Crystal Chenille.

BOB HINES IS A CAPTAIN WITH WIDE FLY-FISHING EXPERI-
ence. Although he specializes in showing clients the best fishing along
the coast of Rhode Island, he has traveled far and wide in search of good
angling. Bob is also a professional casting instructor and fly designer. Hines's
Simple Cinder Worm is a good example of his creativity.

The cinder worm hatch occurs over muddy bottoms from April through
June. Early in the evening during the full moon, the worms leave the pro-
tective shelter of the bottom and begin swimming to the surface to spawn.
The local gamefish gather for the feast, and this is a good time to use a
weighted cinder worm imitation.

Hines's Simple Cinder Worm, which is little more than two inches long,
has a small amount of lead wire wrapped on the hook shank. Cast this sinking into the swarming worms and let it sink. Retrieve the fly slowly toward
you so it starts to rise, and hold on tight for the strike.

Anglers from the Northeast to the Florida Keys plan fishing trips around
the cinder worm hatch. Even trophy tarpon feast on this easy meal and pro-
vide memorable fly-fishing action. If you'd like to try your hand at catching
a tarpon during the cinder worm emergence, contact a guide specializing
in fly fishing in the Keys. Tie Hines's Simple Cinder Worm, and his Walking Cinder Worm, pack a 12-weight rod, and get ready for some of the best
fishing of your life!

Shark Chum Fly

Hook: Regular saltwater hook, size 3/0.
Thread: Black or red 3/0.
Body: Dark or purple Zonker rabbit strip.

IS THE FISHING SLOW BUT YOU WANT TO FEEL A TUG AT THE end of your line? Would you like to feel a really strong tug; would that get your interest? Then perhaps you should spend a day fishing for sharks.

Although not widely practiced, shark fishing is great fun. It is practiced on both the East and West Coasts, so there are plenty of opportunities to catch these fascinating creatures.

I suspect most anglers haven't fished for sharks because a seaworthy boat is required. In some areas, you only have to motor a few hundred yards to reach sharks; in other locations, such as my home state of Maine, you have to travel up to twenty miles from shore, well over the horizon and out of sight of land. If you own or have access to a good boat, you can easily fish for sharks.

Using chum is the key to attracting sharks. After traveling to a likely destination, turn off the motor and allow the boat to drift. Drop a bag full of chum, which you can obtain at most saltwater bait shops, into the water. The boat will continue drifting and the oily chum slick will spread, attracting any nearby shark.

Use a very stout rod, wire leader, and fly designed to look like a chunk of chum. Chuck Furimsky's Shark Chum Fly, which is simply a rabbit Zonker strip wrapped on the hook shank, is a good example. A wad of feathers lashed to the hook will also work.

When a shark approaches, cast the fly right on its nose. The shark, excited by all the fishy aroma in the water, will grab the fly. Hang on tight: depending upon the species, a shark can weigh from fifty to a couple hundred pounds. They are strong fighters and will give a fine tussle.

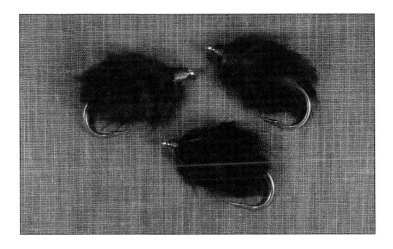

Art's Shrimp

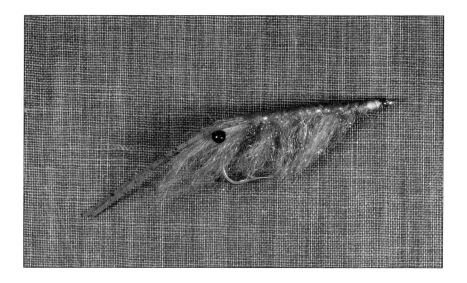

Hook: Long-shank saltwater hook, sizes 8 to 1/0.
Thread: Size 3/0, color to match the body of the fly.
Antennae: Rubber legs to match the color of the body.
Head: A small pinch of dubbing.
Eyes: Melted monofilament.
Body: Shaggy dubbing—tan, pink, or orange. Standard SLF Dubbing is a good choice, but you may select your favorite brand of dubbing.
Back: Thin Skin in a color to match the color of the body.
Rib: 20-pound-test monofilament.

THIS FLY IS NEAR AND DEAR TO MY HEART, AND IT DEFI-
nitely catches fish. I am happy to include it in this book about favorite
saltwater patterns.

Art Scheck was once the editor of *Fly Tyer* magazine. He offered me my
first job in publishing and taught me the ropes of how to be a magazine
editor. He was a very talented author and editor, and also one hell of a fly
designer.

Art created this fly close to twenty years ago. It had no name at the
time—I don't know if Art ever named any of the patterns he designed—so
I call it Art's Shrimp. It has been a part of my fishing kit all these years. It is
great for catching striped bass, and tied in smaller sizes, it is a good candidate
for catching bonefish and redfish. When fishing in Corpus Christi, it was a
top pattern for catching sea trout.

Art's Shrimp is a good candidate for new tiers. The key material is shaggy
dubbing, which you can find in any fly shop. Standard SLF Dubbing is a
good choice, but any similar material will work. You can use a strip of Thin
Skin for tying the shell back, or you may clip a strip from a clear plastic
freezer bag.

Although a lot of shrimp imitations are tied in orange, live shrimp are
usually light tan; shrimp turn orange when cooked. Tie Art's Shrimp in a
similar color to match real shrimp.

RM Shortfin Squid

Head
Thread: White 3/0.
Tentacles and mouth parts: Saddle hackles, Krystal Flash, marabou, and Sili Legs or rubber legs.
Head: Large EZ Body tubing.
Eyes: Extra-large 3D eyes.

Body
Hook: Long-shank saltwater hook, size 4/0.
Thread: Clear monofilament.
Underbody: Chenille, Crystal Chenille, or Cactus Chenille.
Body: Extra-large EZ Body tubing.
Fins: Krystal Flash and marabou.

RICH MURPHY IS A STUDENT OF STRIPED BASS AND HOW to catch them on flies. His book, *Fly Fishing for Striped Bass*, might be the last word on the subject; it is well researched and thorough. Only a master angler could write such a book.

Rich's flies are also well thought out. Here we see his RM Shortfin Squid. Well, actually, Rich didn't tie this fly—I did. I have several in my fly box because they are great for catching striped bass, bluefish, and anything else that feeds on squid.

Real squid are an important part of the diets of many gamefish. There are actually several species of shortfin squids, including the northern shortfin squid. This variety ranges from the Florida Straights to Newfoundland. It is migratory, so you may very well encounter schools of squid and feeding fish.

Tie the head of the RM Shortfin Squid on a heavy needle, such as your bodkin, placed in your tying vise. Tie on the tentacles and mouth parts. Next, remove the bodkin from the vise. Slip a piece of EZ Body tubing over the handle. Tie down the end of the tubing on the base of the head materials. Tie off and clip the thread. Push the tubing back onto the head ingredients. Glue eyes onto the sides of the head. Now you're ready to make the body of the fly.

Place a hook in the vise. Tie on the completed head. Slip a piece of larger tubing over the hook eye. Wrap the chenille underbody, and push the tubing back over the chenille; the completed squid body is actually two layers of tubing, which makes the fly bulletproof. Add the marabou fins and complete the fly.

Tie the RM Shortfin Squid in off-white and tan.

Space Needle

Hook: Regular saltwater hook, size 2.
Thread: Pink 3/0.
Body: Pink chenille tied on Flymen Fishing Company Articulated Fish-Spines.
Tail: Pink marabou.
Eyes: Large 3-D eyes.

THE SPACE NEEDLE IS A COOL IMITATION OF A NEEDLEFISH. This common tropical baitfish lives in shallow marine habitats and is a favorite prey for gamefish such as barracuda. The problem, of course, is preventing sharp-toothed barracuda from slicing the leader and getting away with our flies. Captain Chris Newsome's Space Needle is a fine solution.

Tie the snout of the Space Needle on a long-shank hook with the bend and point removed. Tie the body on a series of interlocking shanks, such as Articulated Fish-Spines. These heavy-duty shanks come in several lengths. Use as many shanks as you wish to create a fly of any length. The Space Needle is tied using a series of short shanks, which makes the fly undulate like a snake. Perhaps the pattern should have been called Space Snake!

A real needlefish has a long snout, which is replicated by wrapping thread on the front hook shank. Coat the head area and the snout of the fly with epoxy. Glue an eye onto each side of the head.

When fishing, the rear hook is several inches from the forward hook eye and the leader. This keeps the mouth of the barracuda well back from the leader. Only an enormous fish—one with the mouth the size of an alligator's—could cut the leader. Chances are you wouldn't want to land that barracuda, anyway!

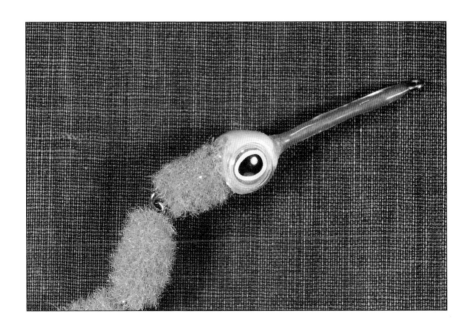

Masked Minnow

Hook: Regular saltwater hook, sizes 4 to 1.
Thread: White 3/0.
Head: Flymen Fishing Company Fish-Mask.
Wing: White and olive bucktail, and pearl Flashabou.
Belly: Pearl Ice Dub.
Eyes: 3D eyes, size to match the Fish-Mask.

ONE OF THE PLEASURES IN WRITING A BOOK SUCH AS THIS is learning about all the new materials being used to design better flies. Sure, I'm including the usual—and expected—Clouser Minnows and Deceivers. Those are favorite patterns and are staples in many fly boxes. But once you've tied or bought enough of those flies, you'll want to know about what is new and fresh.

The Masked Minnow is certainly a new design. At first glance it doesn't seem new, but the lightweight plastic Fish-Mask creating the head gives the pattern a realistic silhouette, and it is easy to make.

Fish-Masks are a product of the Flymen Fishing Company. They slip on the hooks, giving finished baitfish patterns a realistic look. They are also the ideal place to hang eyes, a key trigger for feeding gamefish. Fish-Masks won the best-in-show award for a new fly-tying product at the International Fly Tackle Dealer show in 2013.

Although Flymen Fishing Company sells these light-colored Masked Minnows, you can tie this pattern in your choice of realistic and attractor colors using your choice of natural or synthetic furs and hairs. Simply tie the fly in the normal manner, add a thick drop of cement on the front of the fly, and then slip the Fish-Mask into place. Add the eyes and your pattern is ready for fishing. How simple is that?

Flatfish

Hook: Saltwater jig hook, size 2/0 or 3/0.
Weight: Lead wire.
Body: Leather.
Fins: Grizzly hackle.
Eyes: Medium 3D eyes.

CHUCK FURIMSKY'S FLATFISH IS ONE OF THE MOST UNUsual patterns in this little collection of flies. Even though it looks a little whacky, it really does catch fish!

Chuck spent many years working in the leather goods business. While he specialized in selling clothing, he developed a line of fly-tying products called Bug Skin. It comes in a wide range of colors and textures, and has many applications for designing new patterns.

The Flatfish is an imitation of a baby flounder. A flounder, which lies flat on the ocean in the mud and ambushes its prey, is a fascinating creature. At hatching, a flounder has an eye situated on both sides of its head. As the fish grows from the larval to the juvenile stage of development, one eye migrates to the other side of the head. An adult flounder has both eyes situated on the same side of the head. When at rest, the fish lies on its side with both eyes looking up.

Striped bass feed on flounder, and the Flatfish fly is a good imitation. Making the Flatfish requires no thread. First, wrap lead wire on the hook shank to weight the fly and get it to sink quickly to the bottom; the jig hook will keep the Flatfish turned in the correct position when fishing. Next, cut two pieces of Bug Skin in the shape of a flounder.

Cement the bottom piece of leather to the top of the hook using superglue. Glue a grizzly hackle along each side of the body; the feather stem is on the edges of the leather. Poke a hole in the top half of the body using a bodkin. Thread the hook through the leather, and glue the top half of the body in place.

CHAPTER THREE

Flats Flies:
Patterns for Fishing Skinny Water

Winston Moore's Permit Crab

Hook: Mustad 34007, size 2 or 1.

Thread: Chartreuse 3/0.

Weight: 1/40 ounce or 1/30 ounce nickel-plated dumbbell. The size of dumbbell should match the hook size and depth of water you plan to fish.

Claws and antennae: Furnace brown hackle tips flanked with white marabou, then two strands of Krystal Flash, all equal to one and one-half times the length of the hook shank.

Body: Cream, brown, or tan tufts of wool, clipped from the hide and rolled into bunches.

Legs: White round rubber legs barred with a permanent marker. Tie the legs between the bunches of wool while making the body.

EVEN THOUGH HE HAS CAUGHT WELL MORE THAN 100 permit Winston Moore is one of our sport's unsung permit-fishing masters, and his simple-looking permit fly is the sleeper crab pattern of all time.

After tying sheep's wool to the hook shank, Winston flattens the material into a thin carapace using contact cement to create a body that lands and sinks well. The cement gives the wool a stiff profile that is slightly porous so, with a heavy dumbbell placed at the leading edge of the fly, it slices through the water at an angle and gets down in front of fish a lot faster than other Merkin-style yarn crabs.

Winston shapes the body by pressing contact cement into the wool in stages. And because it takes the cement a while to dry, he continues pressing it into shape while it is hardening; he moistens his fingers in a bowl of water before touching the wool to prevent the glue from sticking to them. Winston ties the fly in cream, brown, and tan.

McFly Crab

Hook: Gamakatsu SC-15, size 1/0.
Thread: Tan 6/0.
Weight: .025 non-lead wire.
Legs and claws: Tan micro Ultra Chenille.
Eyes: Large EP Crab/Shrimp Eyes.
Body: Tan and brown McFly Foam.
Extras: Clear Cure Goo Hydro and tan or off-white fabric paint.

IS IT FAIR TO CALL A FLY "CUTE"? IF IT IS, THEN THE McFLY Crab is very cute. And it's also a fine fishing fly.

Making the McFly Crab requires part tying and part construction techniques. First, wrap a small amount of wire around the hook shank. Next, tie on the legs and claws using short pieces of Ultra Chenille. Lightly melt the tips of the chenille using a cigarette lighter so the material does not unravel when fishing. Now you're ready to craft the body of the fly.

McFly Foam is typically used for making egg patterns and the heads on Wool-Head Sculpins. McFly Foam isn't actually foam, but a type of yarn. It comes in a rainbow of colors so you can use it to tie dozens of different patterns. On the McFly Crab, tie the yarn to the hook and clip the shell body to shape. Glue the eyes to the bottom of the body using light-cured acrylic or epoxy. Color the adhesive using off-white or light tan fabric paint.

Even with a few wraps of lead wire on the hook shank, the McFly Crab is lightweight and lands softly. It is the ideal pattern for fishing to wary bonefish in shallow water. It is also a good choice for casting to redfish and other species of fish that eat crabs.

Hochner's Defiant Crab

Hook: Regular saltwater hook, sizes 6 to 2.
Thread: Chartreuse 3/0.
Weight: Medium lead dumbbell.
Head: Calftail hair and pearl Krystal Flash.
Claws: Badger hackle.
Eyes: Beads of epoxy on monofilament, or small beads glued to the ends of monofilament.
Body: Stiff rug yarn or a similar material.
Legs: Sili Legs.

WOW, WHAT A PATTERN! AT FIRST GLANCE, HOCHNER'S Defiant Crab seems unusual. Most crab imitations are flat, but the body on this pattern is semicircular. Why?

When resting on the bottom, the dumbbell eyes force the nose of the fly down, and the head and claws raise up into a fighting, defiant position. Give the fly gentle strips, and the nose cocks up and the head dips, making the Defiant Crab look as though it is fleeing. Lex Hochner, from Texas, hit upon a great idea when designing this unique pattern.

The Defiant Crab is a fine pattern for catching permit and redfish. Many anglers would consider it a tad heavy and large for bonefish, but you can tie it in smaller sizes and experiment with bonefish.

Lex says most flats anglers fish their flies too slowly for permit. Rather than making short strips, he prefers stripping the line from the bottom guide to the reel seat. In addition to being the best correct length, this method will keep you in firm contact with the fly. Too many anglers don't even know permit have eaten their flies and they miss fish.

Here we see the tan Defiant Crab, which is fine for fishing over sand flats. Be sure to make this fly in olive and brown to fish over other colors of flats.

Miheve's Flats Fly

Hook: Regular saltwater hook, sizes 8 to 2.
Thread: Tan 6/0.
Eyes: Small silver bead chain.
Tail: Tan calftail hair and pearl Krystal Flash.
Body: Tan D Rib.
Body hackle: Tan saddle hackle.
Weed guard: Stiff 20-pound-test monofilament.

A PATTERN DESIGNER NAMED GREG MIHEVE CREATED THIS nifty little bonefish fly. And although Miheve's Flats Fly was designed as a bonefish pattern, it is also a good choice for casting to skittish permit and redfish.

Over the years I have become particularly fond of sparse flies such as Miheve's Flats Fly. Like many tiers creating their first bonefish flies, my patterns were too dense and had too much material. As a result, they hit the water too hard and spooked fish. I started looking in the fly boxes of far more experienced bonefish anglers and noticed my flies were too bushy— almost clunky.

Miheve's Flats Fly is very sparse and appears as just a wisp of fleeing bait when stripped through the water. Given the splayed calftail hair tail, I suspect the fish mistake it for a small shrimp or some other crustacean inhabiting the flats.

When researching Miheve's Flats Fly, I tripped onto a website called DIY Bonefishing. It's a fine resource of anglers eager to plan their own bonefishing trip. This website lists Miheve's Flats Fly as one of its favorite patterns for the do-it-yourself angler. I would also say that it is a good fly for new tiers looking for a simple, fish-catching pattern. The key is to tie it sparse. Use too much material and you'll create one of those overdressed flies that brought me so much disappointment.

Detonator Crab

Hook: Gamakatsu SC15 or similar saltwater hook, size 2/0.
Thread: Blue Danville Flat Waxed Nylon 210.
Eyes: Black extra-large EP Crab/Shrimp Eyes.
Mouth parts and head: Tan Krystal Flash, tan grizzly marabou, and olive Polar Chenille.
Claws: Light brown rabbit Zonker strip.
Body: Mutton snapper EP Fiber 3-D, and olive and tan marabou.
Legs: Pumpkin Fly Enhancer Legs.
Adhesive: Clear Cure Goo Hydro and tack-free Flex.
More stuff: Red, orange, and blue permanent marker.

DREW CHICONE IS ONE OF THE NEW YOUNG GUNS OF FLY tying and fishing. He is a promising fly pattern designer, good writer, and fine photographer. His enthusiasm is contagious, and he is very eager to share what he knows about flies, materials, and fishing. With guys like Drew working at the vise, fly tying has a very bright future.

Drew conceived of the Detonator Crab while fishing for tarpon in the Florida Keys. As he tells the story, "A tennis ball–sized crab caught my attention as it passed the boat in the water beneath my feet. My focus was immediately drawn to the vibrant shades of blues and reds that outlined its legs and claws. Two tarpon approached the boat, and I saw the first fish gracefully gulp the crab from the surface."

While many tiers go to great lengths to design crab imitations featuring stiff shells, Drew created a fly that emphasizes an irresistable swimming action in the water. The claws of the Detonator Crab are rabbit Zonker strips stiffened with Clear Cure Goo or a similar light-cured adhesive, but the rest of the pattern is tied using soft materials: marabou, EP Fibers, and rubber legs.

In addition to tarpon, cast the Detonator Crab to bonefish, redfish, striped bass, and any other species of gamefish that feed on crabs.

Mosquito Lagoon Special

Hook: Mustad 3407, size 6.
Thread: Brown 3/0.
Eyes: Small lead dumbbell.
Wing: Red squirrel tail hair and long strands of copper or gold Krystal Flash.
Head: Deer hair natural.

ORLANDO IS ONE OF NORTH AMERICA'S FAVORITE vacation destinations. Within an hour is some of the best saltwater fishing in the United States. This area is home to Captain John Kumiski.

Captain Kumiski designed the Mosquito Lagoon Special. Mosquito Lagoon is rich in opportunities to fish for tarpon, redfish, lady fish, crevalle jack, and more.

Mosquito Lagoon is one of the least developed regions on the east coast of Florida. A large part of the area is protected in the Mosquito Lagoon Aquatic Preserve. When visiting, keep your eye peeled for the resident population of Atlantic bottlenose dolphins.

In addition to using a boat, Captain Kumiski takes more adventuresome anglers fishing using kayaks. These small craft are ideal for accessing narrow backwaters and exploring areas that see few anglers. It's also a great way to get close to the local crocodiles. In addition to kayaking the backwaters surrounding Mosquito Lagoon, Captain Kumiski kayaks the Everglades in search of good fishing.

Captain Kumiski prefers using natural materials when designing many of his patterns. The Mosquito Lagoon Special, which features squirrel tail and deer hair, is typical of his flies. It is a fine pattern for catching redfish and other species that feed on the flats. This is also a good pattern for novice tiers because all fly shops carry inexpensive materials. The deer hair makes the fly suspend in the water so it is easily visible to the fish.

EZ Slider

Hook: Regular saltwater hook, size 6.
Thread: Black 6/0.
Eyes: Small lead dumbbell.
Tail: Tan Polar Fiber, craft fur, or your favorite synthetic hair.
Body: Brown Crystal Chenille.
Body hackle: Grizzly.

CAPTAIN JOHN KUMISKI CREATES STRAIGHTFORWARD fishing flies: basic materials, basic designs—excellent results. The EZ Slider is one of his typical patterns.

You'll find all the materials you need to tie the EZ Slider at your local fly shop. Although this is the tan version of this pattern, you can tie it in white, chartreuse, or any other color. The tan EZ Slider, however, is perfect for fishing sand flats for bonefish, redfish, and sea trout. You could fill half a fly box with this simple pattern in an evening and be ready to take the saltwater flats by storm.

Note the barring on the synthetic tail. Few things in nature are one solid color. Almost all natural baits exhibit a variety of colors, often masking them from predators. Captain Kumiski adds bars to the tail of the EZ Slider using a permanent marker. This is a common technique that makes the fly look somewhat like a small baitfish when retrieved through the water. Use markers to add bars and spots to many flies tied with synthetic wings and tails.

The EZ Slider is a fairly lightweight pattern. Although it is tied with a small dumbbell, it lands gently and rarely spooks fish. Let the fly sink to the sand and allow the fish to approach. When the fish get within a couple of feet of the pattern, tighten your line and raise the fly off the bottom as though it is a piece of fleeing bait. The fish will bust forward and inhale it.

Cathy's Fleeing Crab

Hook: Mustad 34007, sizes 4 to 1.

Thread: Chartreuse 3/0.

Weight: Metal dumbbell—small for hook size 4, medium for size 2, or large for size 1.

Tail: White over orange marabou.

Body: Tan Sea Fibers or EP Fibers.

Legs and wing: Fire-tip clear/orange Sili Legs.

CATHY AND BARRY BECK ARE TWO OF OUR BEST-KNOWN fly fishers. They are superb photographers, great teachers, and just fine people. I met them close to thirty years ago at a fly-fishing show in Carlyle, Pennsylvania, when they owned a fly shop, and I still see them from time to time.

Not many people know that the Becks are also talented fly designers. Although they spend a good deal of time fishing for trout on the Keystone State's limestone streams, they also lead groups of anglers around the world in search of good saltwater angling.

This imitation is called Cathy's Fleeing Crab. It is an excellent flats pattern for catching bonefish and permit. The Fleeing Crab sinks quickly, and its long silicone legs come alive as it drops through the water column. Its bicolor marabou tail helps the Fleeing Crab attract fish even when the fly is stationary.

The Fleeing Crab is considered a good choice for catching a grand slam where permit and bonefish share the flats. In addition to tan, tie Cathy's Fleeing Crab in olive and brown to match dark-colored flats.

If you ever see the Becks, be sure to stop and say hello. You'll be glad you met these nice people.

Dick's Phantom Permit Crab

Hook: Gamakatsu SL-12 or Mustad 34007, size 2 or 1.

Thread: Orange 3/0.

Weight: Plain dumbbell—small (1/30 ounce) for hook size 2, or large (1/20 ounce) for size 1.

Flash (optional): Two short strands orange Krystal Flash.

Egg sac: Orange rabbit hair.

Eyes: Melted monofilament.

Legs: Two short tan/black or white/black grizzly-barred round rubber legs.

Body: Fluorescent orange and tan blended dubbing, combed toward the hook bend and flattened.

Carapace: Steve Farrar's Flash Blend (mullet brown and off-white) tied at hook eye, brushed flat, and trimmed to shape.

DICK BROWN IS A LEADING SALTWATER ANGLER. HE TRAVELS the world in search of good fishing, and he uses his experiences to design better flies. Fortunately for us, he describes his patterns and how to fish them in magazine articles and two highly respected books.

This is his Phantom Permit Crab. Dick says he designed this fly with an "angular, streamlined profile" so that it drops quickly through the water column "faster than just about any crab pattern I've used." Dick also says that the soft fiber carapace lands on the water more quietly than conventional round- and oval-shaped crab imitations.

Dick really poured it on when he created his Phantom Permit Crab. The pattern includes monofilament stalks for extended eyes, soft rabbit hair for mouthparts, rubber legs, and orange rabbit hair for an egg sac.

After tying the body, Dick says you can use a fine-toothed comb to smooth out and align the Flash Blend fibers, and then press a small amount of head cement or GOOP into the fibers to flatten and fix them into the fan-shaped carapace.

The Kwan

Hook: Tiemco 800s or Mustad 34007, sizes 2 to 1/0.
Thread: Brown 3/0.
Weight: Lead dumbbell sized to suit the desired sink rate.
Tail: Tan Fly Fur or Polar Fibre barred with a brown permanent marker.
Tail support: Stiff deer hair fibers tied on at the bottom and top of the hook bend to keep the tail from fouling.
Body: Alternating brown and tan rug or acrylic yarn.

PATRICK DORSEY IS AN EXPERT AT FISHING THE FLATS, AND he fishes in permit tournaments in the Florida Keys. He created the Kwan, a universally popular pattern, and says it is one of his best patterns for catching permit. The Kwan is also an ideal fly for catching a grand slam of a permit, bonefish, and tarpon.

Tying the Kwan is fairly straightforward. Use stiff yarn—rug yarn is a favorite material—for making the body of the fly. Tie strands of yarn—single or alternating colors—to the hook shank using figure-eight wraps. Clip the body to shape, and add a bead of cement on the thread wraps to lock the yarn to the hook.

The tail is Fly Fur, Polar Fibre, or even just craft fur. Don't overdress the tail; keep it sparse and willowy so it swims and waves with the slightest twitch of the line. Most tiers add bars to the tail using permanent marker.

Flats fly-fishing authority Dick Brown tied this version of the Kwan for catching permit. If you are targeting bonefish, you should scale the pattern down and tie it on hook sizes 8 and 4.

Palometa Crab

Hook: Mustad 34007, sizes 4 to 1.

Thread: Chartreuse 3/0.

Weight: Metal dumbbell—small (1/40 ounce) for hook size 4, medium (1/30 ounce) for size 2, or large (1/20 ounce) for size 1.

Tail and claws: Chartreuse marabou flanked by a pair of grizzly hackle tips.

Body: Strands of tan EP Fibers. Sprinkle very short, finely cut pieces of EP Fibers on top of the finished carapace (brushed with head cement) for added realism.

Legs and wing: Black and white barred round rubber legs.

THIS MODIFIED DERIVATIVE OF THE MERKIN AND RAG Head is a favorite of the Punta Allen and Ascension Bay areas; it has evolved with some tweaking by the local guides in this great permit fishery. Its strongly barred legs and chartreuse tail create essential triggering elements that give it a well-deserved reputation for delivering the goods on the toughest days. Gluing shorts strands of EP Fibers onto the carapace with a bit of head cement has a hardening effect similar to the contact cement used on Moore's Permit Crab, giving the Palometa Crab a sleeker profile and faster sink rate.

Bastard Permit Crab

Hook: Mustad 34007, size 2 or 1.
Thread: Fluorescent pink 3/0.
Weight: Dumbbell—medium (1/30 ounce) for hook size 2, or large (1/20 ounce) for size 1.
Tail: Clump of pale tan or cream marabou.
Body: Tan EP Fibers.
Legs and wing: Sand/orange flake Sili Legs.

AARON ADAMS'S BASTARD CRAB IS ONE OF MY FAVORITE bonefish patterns, and when tied in larger sizes and properly weighted, it has also become a major permit fly. Its long, staggered Sili Legs trail the fly when stripped, and like Cathy Beck's Fleeing Crab, they flutter on the drop. Tie this fly in tan, cream, or olive. The semitransparent legs give this pattern subtler animation than many other crab flies. The tail should be full rather than sparse, extending beyond the bend a distance equal to slightly more than the length of the hook shank.

To build the body, roll a bunch of EP Fibers between your fingers so they form a strand equal to the diameter of a piece of yarn. Cut the strands into short pieces about 1 inch long. Tie the short strands to the hook using figure-eight wraps. Tie the legs on the hook-point side of the body, straddling the shank and angling back toward the hook point.

Avalon Permit Fly

Hook: Tiemco 811S or Mustad 34007, size 2.
Thread: Tan 3/0.
Eyes: Silver or gold 1/8-inch dumbbell.
Keel: 20-pound-test hard nylon monofilament and four 7/64-inch-diameter silver or stainless-steel beads.
Mouth: Arctic fox tail dyed orange, 3/8-inch long.
Antennae: Black Krystal Flash, about 2 ¾-inches long.
Legs: Two strands of medium orange/black grizzly barred rubber legs.
Shellback: Two strands of pearl flat Diamond Braid.
Body: Tan marabou, wrapped on the hook and trimmed.
Claws: Two light tan Zonker strips tied delta-wing style.
Head: Fluorescent orange thread (210-denier).

CREATED AT CUBA'S AVALON FLY FISHING CENTER, THIS novel design captures the profile of a large shrimp and employs a keel-weighted device so it lands and remains right side up. The unique monofilament-strung beads that serve as weights also make tiny clicking sounds to attract fish.

With its rear-facing profile, the Avalon Permit Fly presents several enticing triggers to fish including long legs, antennae, and mouthparts, but perhaps the most inviting trigger is its pair of wavy rabbit-fur claws. Not only is the appearance of the fly a radical departure from other permit flies, its track record is remarkable: it has taken more than 450 permit since it was introduced in 2009!

You can add this method of stringing beads to a great many permit and larger bonefish patterns. It is a unique approach and points to the willingness of saltwater fly tiers to innovate and break any established ideas about what makes a proper fly.

Bone Appetite

Hook: Regular saltwater hook, size 6 or 4.
Thread: Orange 3/0.
Tail: Pearl Krystal Flash.
Body: Orange tying thread and pearl Krystal Flash.
Wing: Tan rabbit fur and silver-speckled clear Sili Legs.
Eyes: Small silver dumbbell.

THE BONE APPETITE IS A TERRIFIC PATTERN FOR NOVICE tiers. Any fly shop worthy of its name will have all the ingredients, and learning to make it is easy. Getting the hang of the proportions is the only snag; beginning tiers tend to overdress their flies.

First, tie on the dumbbell eyes on top of the hook shank and well back from the hook eye; this forces the fly to flip over in the water so it doesn't snag the bottom. Use about eight strands of Krystal Flash for the tail of the Bone Appetite. Do not clip the long extra portion of the Krystal Flash; save this for wrapping over the thread body. Make a level thread body, and then wrap the Krystal Flash. The small tuft of rabbit fur and Sili Legs give the Bone Appetite good swimming action.

Don't let the name of the Bone Appetite fool you. Use this fly to catch bonefish, but it is also a killer permit pattern. It would also be one of my first choices when casting to redfish. Actually, the Bone Appetite will catch any flats fish that feed on small shrimp and crustaceans.

For a little variety, switch thread colors to tie other versions of the Bone Appetite. You might also select other colors of rabbit fur and Sili Legs. Tie the Bone Appetite in olive, light olive, and tan. And, you can substitute with lighter small bead-chain eyes to create a selection of flies for fishing especially skinny water.

Bonefish Slider

Hook: Mustad 34007, sizes 8 to 2.
Thread: Flat Wax Nylon.
Eyes: Small lead dumbbell.
Tail: Craft fur.
Collar: Saddle hackle.
Head: Deer body hair.

THE BONEFISH SLIDER WAS CREATED BY TIM BORSKI. TIM grew up in Stevens Point, Wisconsin, spending time ice fishing. When in his twenties he moved to Miami, and eventually to the Florida Keys. Today, Tim makes his home in Islamorada.

Although Tim has created several terrific patterns over the years, he is probably better known as a fine artist. Tim works in oils and acrylics. His subjects are mostly the fish and wildlife he sees in the Keys, but other paintings depict striped bass, Mongolian trout, taimen, marlin, and birds not commonly seen in Florida. One of his greatest honors was to be included in an article for *Men's Journal* magazine. This article had nothing to do with fishing; it was about unusual characters living in the Keys.

In the recipe for the Bonefish Slider, I elected not to include colors for the various materials. A regular Bonefish Slider is tied in tan, but you can also make it in chartreuse, black, olive, or any other color. Although it was originally used to catch bonefish, it is also fine for catching redfish and sea trout.

The Bonefish Slider is easy to tie, but don't over-tie it with too much material; the best Slider is sparse and wispy. Add bars on the tail using a brown or black permanent marker. The tail makes the fly look alive when stripped through the water.

Merkin Crab

Hook: Regular saltwater hook, size 6 to 1/0.
Thread: Chartreuse 3/0.
Eyes: Small lead dumbbell.
Tail: Barred ginger hackles and pearl Flashabou.
Body: Light tan rug yarn.
Legs: Rubber legs.

PERMIT ARE EXTREMELY DIFFICULT TO CATCH; SOME anglers spend many thousands of dollars and hundreds of hours pursuing this top-notch gamefish. The Merkin Crab, designed by angler Del Merkin, is one of the most famous flies for catching wary permit.

The small dumbbell eyes encourage the hook to flip over so the fly fishes with the point on top so the Merkin does not snag on the bottom. The long rubber legs give the Merkin excellent action and suggest a fleeing crab.

Make the body of the Merkin using rug yarn; common cotton and other soft-fibered yarns are not suitable for this fly. Rug yarn is stiff so the fly holds its shape. Tie strands of yarn to the hook, and clip the body to shape. I have given the recipe for a tan-colored crab, but many anglers tie olive Merkins for fishing on marl and weedy flats. I have also seen Merkins tied using alternating colors of rug yarn, such as tan and light brown; perhaps the slight barring gives these flies a more realistic appearance.

Does the original Merkin look like a crab? Not to me, but beauty is in the eye of the beholder. To permit and bonefish, the round flat profile and swimming legs is enough to convince them that the Merkin is something good to eat.

Here is my version of the Merkin. I selected alternating colors of tan and brown rug yarn for the body, and brown rubber legs. I have caught many fish using this color combination. Remember: pattern recipes are just suggestions. Just like when following a cooking recipe, you can change ingredients to please your own taste.

Bob's Mantis Shrimp

Hook: Mustad 34007, sizes 6 to 1.

Thread: Tan 3/0.

Weight: Lead dumbbell, small (1/40 ounce) or medium (1/30 ounce).

Antennae: Two strands of black Krystal Flash.

Eyes: 80-pound-test melted monofilament painted with black fingernail polish.

Rostrum/head (tail of fly): Tan craft fur.

Mouthparts: A tuft of tan rabbit fur cut from the hide and equal to one-third the length of the rostrum.

Body: Tan dubbing.

Legs: Sili Legs.

IT'S IMPOSSIBLE TO PIGEONHOLE BOB VEVERKA. HE WROTE one of the best books about how to tie Spey flies, the beautiful patterns originated on Scotland's River Spey. Before that he wrote a terrific book titled *Innovative Saltwater Flies*. Along the way, his patterns—salmon, saltwater, and trout—have appeared in articles and books written by other authors.

This is Bob's imitation of a Mantis shrimp. You can tie this pattern in a smaller size 6 for catching bonefish, or sizes 2 and 1 for permit. Bob's Mantis is especially popular in the Bahamas.

Mantis shrimp are curious creatures. They are members of the order Stomatopoda. Mantis sometimes reach 12 inches in length, but of course we do not tie flies to imitate these large shrimp. They are common on tropical and subtropical flats, but we only recently began understanding them because they spend most of their lives hiding in burrows and holes. When smaller Mantis shrimp do appear, however, bonefish and permit eagerly feed on them. Mantis shrimp have strong claws that they use to spear, stun, and dismember their prey.

Bob's Mantis has a lot of built-in movement. Almost any pattern tied using rabbit fur will catch fish, and Bob uses this soft material for the head and mouth. The body is dubbing, which is also soft and creates a lifelike fly. And finally, the rubber legs make the pattern look alive when stripped through the water.

Rocket Man Mantis

Hook: Mustad 34007, sizes 4 to 1.

Thread: Chartreuse 3/0.

Weight: Nickel-plated lead barbell, select a size to achieve the desired sink rate; typically 1/40 or 1/30 ounce.

Eyes: Two strands 80-pound-test melted monofilament painted with orange or black fingernail polish.

Antennae: Two strands black Krystal Flash.

Rostrum/mouthparts: Chartreuse rabbit hair cut from the hide.

Egg sac and underbody: Orange sparkle yarn.

Legs and claws: Two pairs of splayed Sili Legs, fire tipped orange/clear or your choice of color.

Body: Watery olive Wapsi SLF Saltwater Dubbing, spun in a dubbing loop.

Wing/carapace: Olive Polar Fibre or craft fur, then two strands pearl Krystal Flash.

THE ROCKET MAN IS PATTERNED AFTER SAMPLES OF THE
scurrying rock mantises that inhabit coral and rubble bottoms. It includes
seven visual triggers—eyes, antennae, working mandible, forelegs, egg sac,
inner glow, and pulsating thorax—to entice permit. Most of these stimula-
tors come alive after the drop even when the fly is stationary, a definite plus
with these picky fish. When you fish the Rocket Man Mantis, be sure to let
these tantalizers do their thing. You can tie a bright version of this pattern
with chartreuse thread, a dull version with olive thread, and a spawning version with an orange egg sac.

Gotcha

Hook: Regular saltwater hook, sizes 8 to 2.
Thread: Tan or pink 6/0.
Eyes: Small stainless-steel bead chain or extra-small lead dumbbell.
Tail: Pearl Mylar tubing.
Body: Pearl Body Braid.
Wing: Craft fur and a couple of strands of Krystal Flash.

THE GOTCHA IS ONE OF THE BEST-PRODUCING BONEFISH flies ever created. It is easy to tie, lands softly, and rides with the hook point on top so it doesn't snag grass.

The Gotcha is an ideal selection when you want a small fly with a little flash. The tail is Mylar tubing picked out and frayed. Tie the butt end of the tubing the entire length of the body to create a level underbody. Pearl Body Braid is commonly used for making the body of the Gotcha, but this material also comes in a variety of dyed colors; tan and or light brown matches a real shrimp. Once you master the basics of making this pattern, you might want to add narrow barring to the wing using a brown or black permanent marker.

Craft fur, used for the wing, is very soft and has a realistic swimming action in the water. You'll find this material in a wide variety of colors; white, pink, and orange are popular, but light olive and tan are also good choices.

Most Gotchas are tied with small stainless-steel bead-chain eyes to create flies that land gently and do not spook the fish. But, for fishing deeper water, you can tie Gotchas using extra-small lead dumbbells. And for fishing extremely shallow water, you might want to carry a few Gotchas with no eyes at all!

In addition to bonefish, the Gotcha is a fine redfish, permit, and speckled trout pattern. The Gotcha has wide application, so you will want to carry a few of these flies in your fishing kit.

Crazy Charlie

Hook: Regular saltwater hook, sizes 8 to 4.
Thread: Size 6/0, color to complement the wing.
Body: Silver, gold, or pearl tinsel, and clear medium D-Rib.
Eyes: Small bead chain.
Wing: White, tan, pink, or chartreuse calftail.

THE CRAZY CHARLIE IS CONSIDERED A CLASSIC BONEFISH pattern. Many anglers cut their teeth fishing the flats using the Crazy Charlie, and it is one of the first patterns tiers make when they fill a box full of flies for their first flats-fishing trip. In addition to bonefish, the Crazy Charlie is a fine fly when fishing for redfish and even permit. And it's fairly lightweight, so you can use this pattern and scale down the size of your tackle if you are casting to smaller fish or if the wind drops.

The Crazy Charlie fits into the category of patterns called "attractors." An attractor fly matches nothing specific in nature, but its size, color, and general action convince the fish that it is something good to eat.

Seasoned guides say that your flies should match the color of the flats you plan to fish, and this is easily accomplished with the Crazy Charlie. Change the color of the wing to match the flats you will visit. Favorite colors for Crazy Charlies are white and tan for fishing over light-colored, sandy bottoms, and light olive and olive for marl flats.

Some calftails have curly hair, but I prefer tails with slightly straighter hair. Also, don't overdress the wing on the Crazy Charlie; a small bunch of hair is ample to make a nice fly.

Bonefish Bitters

Hook: Regular saltwater hook, sizes 8 and 6.
Thread: Tan or olive 6/0.
Head: Small bead chain coated with epoxy or fabric paint.
Legs: Tan or olive rubber or Sili Legs.
Wing: Pearl Krystal Flash and deer or elk hair.

EVER SINCE CRAIG MATHEWS DEVELOPED THE BONEFISH Bitters for fishing Belize's Turneffe Island, it has become one of the most popular flats flies in the world. It's very easy to tie, and catches fish even when it's at rest; the bonefish see this stylized crab sitting on the sand or coral, and they snatch it.

I discovered this pattern when preparing for my first trip to Turneffe Island. The lodge, Turneffe Flats, included it on the list of recommended patterns for catching bonefish. It looked simple to tie and could be made in a variety of colors, so I made a dozen or more in olive and tan. The "Bitters," as the locals call it, is very lightweight and perfect for casting with a lighter rod; Belize bonefish run on the small side, and you can scale back the size of your tackle if the wind is calm.

A lot of anglers dream of fishing Turneffe Island, and I will give you another tip: Carry plenty of flies. Many of the best flats are sharp coral that can slice through a leader, and you will lose fish and flies. But, there are herds of bonefish, and they are easy to catch.

Sometimes this pattern is called Pops Bonefish Bitters, in honor of Winston "Pops" Cabral, one of the favorite guides at Turneffe Flats. I spent a week fishing with "Pops," and he recommended a very simple technique: when a school of bonefish approaches, cast the fly several feet in front of the fish and let it settle to the bottom. Next, wait for the school to pass over the fly and the line to tighten, a sure sign that a fish has picked up your fly.

Merkwan Permit Fly

Hook: Mustad 34007, sizes 6 to 2.

Thread: Fluorescent pink 3/0.

Eyes: Lead dumbbell sized to suit the desired sink rate; typically 1/40 or 1/30 ounce.

Tail: Tan craft fur barred with a black permanent marker.

Body: Brown and tan EP Fibers.

THE BONEFISH & TARPON TRUST'S AARON ADAMS CREATED the Merkwan. It is named for its marriage of two of our best permit flies, the Merkin and the Kwan. The Merkwan gives us a subtle alternative to leggy crab-style flies by substituting a barred craft-fur tail for the usual trailing swimming legs. This is among the easiest and quickest of permit patterns to tie.

Roll EP Fibers between your fingers so they look like a strand of yarn. Tie on strands of rolled fibers perpendicular to the hook shank, just as you would when making a standard Merkin. Clip the body to shape and complete the fly.

The Bonefish & Tarpon Trust, based in Key Largo, Florida, is a leading organization researching and protecting our marine environment. The BTT deserves all of our support.

Turneffe Crab

Hook: Tiemco TMC811S, size 8 or 6.
Thread: Tan 6/0.
Eyes: Small lead dumbbell.
Body: Furry Foam.
Legs: Rubber legs.
Back: Deer hair.

THE TURNEFFE CRAB IS SOMETIMES CALLED THE BELIZE
Crab.

Every year, hundreds—probably thousands—of anglers visit Belize to
enjoy this small Central American country's fine fishing. Belize borders
the Caribbean and offers opportunities to catch snook, tarpon, permit, and
bonefish.

Belize is at the top of the list of fishing destinations for many new saltwater fly fishermen. Although most of the bonefish are not large—travel to
the Bahamas or the Florida Keys if you must have big bonefish—you will
encounter large schools of bonefish in Belize. It would be a tough trip if
you spent a few days on the flats around Turneffe Island, off the coast of
Belize, and did not catch a few bonefish.

The schools of bonefish are so large that most guides advise you to cast
your fly several feet ahead of the roving fish, let the school move over your
fly, and wait until a bonefish simply plucks it up. The greatest challenge is
preventing the fish from tangling your line around one of the many large
coral heads; these sharp features easily cut through a monofilament leader.
It's heartbreaking to hook a nice fish and suddenly feel the line go limp.

The Turneffe Crab is simple to tie. It is a fine, basic crab imitation that
will catch fish in many parts of the world. Tie the fly in tan and olive to
match the colors of the flats and crabs whereever you fish.

UV2 Shrimp

Hook: Regular saltwater hook, sizes 8 to 4.
Thread: Tan 3/0.
Weight: Small chrome dumbbell.
Tail: Tan craft fur and pearl Krystal Flash.
Eyes: Melted monofilament.
Mouth: A small tuft of tan UV2 Scud and Shrimp Dubbing.
Body: Tan UV2 Scud and Shrimp Dubbing.
Legs: Clear Sili Legs.

THE UV2 SHRIMP IS A SIMPLE IMITATION OF A REAL SHRIMP that has a lot to recommend it.

First, the UV2 Shrimp is very easy to make. First tie the dumbbell to the top of the hank so the hook flips over when fishing and the fly is less likely to snag the bottom. Tie on the tail and mouth, and then spin a pinch of dubbing on the thread. Tie on the legs while wrapping the dubbing up the hook shank. The key is to make the fly sparse; the UV2 Shrimp should appear slightly transparent in the water like a real shrimp.

UV2 Scud and Shrimp Dubbing is a product of a fly-tying materials company called Spirit River. According to Spirit River, fish have the ability to see colors in the ultraviolet wavelength that we cannot see, and fish more easily see flies tied using materials processed with their exclusive ultraviolet light treatment. Does this really work?

I have heard from many anglers who insist that they are catching more fish using flies with UV2 ingredients: feathers, furs, dubbing, and more. In one report, anglers used the same patterns on the same water to catch striped bass; the only difference was that some flies were tied using UV2 materials, and others were made using non-treated ingredients. The UV2 flies definitely caught more bass.

Salt Creature

Hook: Regular saltwater hook, size 4.
Thread: Tan 6/0.
Tail: Tan Sili Legs or rubber legs.
Body: Tan Crystal Chenille or Cactus Chenille.
Head: Small Flymen Fishing Company Baitfish Head.

THE FLYMEN FISHING COMPANY IS A LEADING INNOVATIVE
fly-tying materials outfit based in North Carolina. Martin Bawden, the head
honcho at the Flymen Fishing Company, is also coming up with fresh materials and patterns. His booth at the fly-fishing shows is always full of tiers
eager to learn what is new, and how they can make better fish-catching
flies.

The Salt Creature is one of Martin's patterns. It is designed for catching bonefish and redfish, but it also attracts sea trout and permit. Is it an
imitation of a shrimp? Who knows! What matters is that the fish think it is
something good to eat.

The Baitfish Head, a product of Flymen Fishing Company, is the key
feature of this fly. The head adds weight and eyes to the fly. (Okay, with
those eyes, the Salt Creature probably doesn't imitate a shrimp.) First, tie on
the monofilament weed guard. Slip the Baitfish Head onto the hook and
into position, and then tie the tail and body.

This is a lightweight Salt Creature suitable for casting to bonefish and
redfish in especially skinny water. Tie the Salt Creature using a medium-
size Baitfish Head for making a fly for catching permit and other species in
slightly deeper water. This heavier fly will sink more quickly, and the slight
splash from the extra weight should not spook the fish.

Ghost

Hook: Regular saltwater hook, size 6.
Thread: Clear monofilament.
Tail: Tan rabbit fur fibers plucked from hide and two strands pink shrimp Krystal Flash.
Eyes: Melted monofilament.
Body: Tan and pink Enrico Puglisi's Shrimp Dub or SLF Saltwater Dubbing.

THIS IS ONE OF DICK BROWN'S FAVORITE PATTERNS FOR catching bonefish. Dick is a leading authority on catching these elusive fish, and has written and lectured about the subject for many years. His book, *Fly Fishing for Bonefish*, is mandatory reading for anyone interested in this subject. Whether you are planning your first trip to the flats, or have chased bonefish for many seasons, you will learn something from this outstanding volume.

The Ghost is a lightweight, wispy pattern. It lands very gently so it will not spook fish, and the rabbit fur tail gives the fly excellent swimming action in the water. Whether dropping through the water or on the retrieve, the Ghost looks alive.

The Ghost is also economical and easy to make. You'll find the ingredients at almost any fly shop. If your local shop doesn't stock the recommended dubbings, you may substitute with another brand of fine-fibered saltwater dubbing. Tying the fly sparse is the key; do not overdress the Ghost. The goal is to create a shadowy fly that suggests life. The fish will think the fly is a shrimp or some other form of crustacean living on the flat. Dick says it is one of his favorite patterns for catching tailing bonefish, and that it works especially well for skittish fish. He recommends fishing the Ghost using short strips.

Reverend Laing

Hook: Regular saltwater hook, sizes 8 to 4.
Thread: White 6/0.
Eyes: Small dumbbell.
Tail: Pearl Midge Flash or Krystal Flash.
Body: Pearl braided tinsel.
Wing: Natural Kinky Fibre and root beer Midge Flash or Krystal Flash.

THE REVEREND LAING IS ANOTHER BONEFISH PATTERN recommended by fly-fishing authority Dick Brown. It is a collaboration of David Skok and Jaime Boyle. I've introduced David elsewhere in this book, so let me tell you about Jaime.

Captain Jaime Boyle offers fly and light-tackle fishing trips on the waters surrounding Martha's Vineyard. He specializes in catching striped bass, bluefish, false albacore, bonito, and bluefin tuna. Depending upon the targeted species, he might use a smaller boat to fish in-shore, or step up to a larger craft to fish off-shore. He has been guiding clients for more than twenty years and is expert at finding and catching fish.

When he is not guiding, he might take a trip in search of different and more exotic fish. Change is good, right?

Jaime and David have traveled far and wide in search of good fishing. They also develop new patterns to match the conditions they find. The Reverend Laing is one of their flies. Although it contains nothing new or unusual, it is a fine fish catcher. Dress it sparse, and retrieve with short, gentle strips. Bonefish, redfish, and other inhabitants of the flats will mistake it for a fleeing form of prey and strike. Change the colors of materials—tan and light olive are obvious choices—to match the color of any flat you encounter. The Reverend Laing is an adaptable pattern, and I know it will find a place in your fishing kit.

The Other Crab

Hook: Long-shank saltwater hook, size 6.
Thread: Tan 6/0.
Eyes: Melted monofilament.
Body: Tan grizzly hackle coated with Softex.
Legs and claws: Tan grizzly hackles.

OVER THE YEARS, CAPTAIN TOM MCQUADE HAS SENT samples of his unique and innovative patterns. A native of the mainland, Captain McQuade moved to the Virgin Islands many years ago. He tests and improves his patterns on the waters of his adopted land, but they catch fish around the world.

The Other Crab is a fun little fly. He calls it The Other Crab to distinguish it from his first crab imitation, but he has tied many variations of crabs, so this example could be the second, third, or fourth iteration. But who's counting?

Almost the entire pattern is tied using tan grizzly feather. First, wrap one or two feathers on the hook. Tie off and snip the thread. Clip the fibers from the front, top, and bottom of the fly; the bottom of the fly is actually the top of the hook shank. Next, coat the top of the remaining fibers with Softex or a similar fly-tying adhesive. Pinch the body to bind the fibers together. Allow the adhesive to dry, and cut the edges into the shape of the crab body. Apply a second coat of adhesive, and place the legs and claws in the glue. After the adhesive dries, you may add markings using a waterproof pen. Even without additional markings, The Other Crab is a fine imitation of a tan crab.

Many crabs are weighted to drop to the bottom, but The Other Crab suspends in the water column. Use a slow retrieve to imitate a fleeing crab. This lightweight fly creates little disturbance when it lands and rarely spooks the fish.

Critter Crab

Hook: Regular saltwater hook, size 6.
Thread: White or tan 3/0.
Weight: Small lead dumbbell.
Eyes: Melted monofilament.
Head: Orange Crystal Flash.
Feelers: Tan saddle hackle.
Body: Tan rug yarn.
Weed guard: 25-pound-test stiff monofilament.

THE CRITTER CRAB IS A GREAT OLD PATTERN. IT'S BEEN around for many fishing seasons, and it is still popular. Sure, there are other flies that look more realistic, but this simple concoction of hackle, chenille, and yarn contains everything required for making a fish-catching crab imitation.

The small dumbbell adds just enough weight so the fly drops to the bottom, yet it makes only a very slight splash with touching the water. Tie on the monofilament eyes and chenille head, and then wrap the saddle hackle in front of the head. Brush the hackle fibers toward the rear of the fly, and add a few thread wraps to hold the fibers in place.

The body is tan or gold rug yarn tied perpendicular to the hook shank. This pattern requires only five pieces of yarn. Add the monofilament weed guard, and tie off and snip the thread. I place a thin bead of cement on the thread wraps in the center of the body to weld the yarn to the hook.

Clip the yarn body into the oval shape of a real crab. You can add the Critter Crab to your fly box, or color the back using a light brown or olive permanent marker. Color the fly to match the crabs you are likely to encounter, or tie Critter Crabs in a variety of colors to match any fishing situation. This fly is easy to make so you can quickly create a variety of crab imitations.

Imitator Shrimp

Hook: Regular saltwater hook, size 2.
Thread: Olive 3/0.
Head: A tuft of tan rabbit fur.
Antennae: Pearl Krystal Flash.
Claws: Tan grizzly hackle.
Eyes: Melted monofilament or a plastic dumbbell.
Body: Tying thread.
Rib: Pearl Krystal Flash.
Rattle: A small glass rattle.
Weed guard: 25-pound-test stiff monofilament.

IT'S COMMON TO ADD RATTLES TO LARGER BAITFISH imitations, but rattles do have other applications. In this case, adding a small rattle increases the power of the Imitator Shrimp to attract fish.

The Imitator Shrimp is a fine lightweight, semitransparent pattern that, on its own, does a good job of imitating a real shrimp. Cast the fly, allow it a moment to sink, and then begin a slow stripping retrieve. The small rattle makes just enough noise to help the fish locate the fly.

The Imitator Shrimp is a good choice when fishing for sea trout and redfish, but it will also catch bonefish. It will certainly catch other varieties of shrimp-eating gamefish.

After tying the body and completing the fly, tie off and snip the thread. Glue the rattle to the top of the hook shank using epoxy or a drop of super-glue. Add another drop of cement on the thread body, in front of the rattle, and between the monofilament eyes.

The Imitator Shrimp is a durable pattern, and it is lightweight enough to use on skinny-water flats. Tie this pattern using olive, pink, or tan thread. Changing the color of the thread does have a profound effect on the appearance of the finished fly. You can also use a larger hook and rattle to make bigger versions of the Imitator Shrimp for catching species such as snook and striped bass.

The Thing

Hook: Regular saltwater hook, sizes 8 to 4.
Thread: Clear monofilament.
Head: White calftail hair.
Antennae: Black Krystal Flash.
Feelers: Grizzly Sili Legs.
Eyes: Plastic dumbbell.
Body: Grizzly saddle hackle.
Weed guard: 25-pound-test monofilament.

CAPTAIN TOM MCQUADE'S PATTERN CALLED THE THING has been a top producer in my fly box for many years. This unique little fly looks like nothing in particular, or perhaps it looks like many things. Tom says it is designed to imitate many of the crustaceans living on the flats, and he must be right; I have used The Thing to catch redfish, bonefish, sea trout, and more.

The Thing requires only a couple of common ingredients: calftail, Krystal Flash, rubber legs, and grizzly hackle. Although I have given colors of materials in the pattern recipe, you can easily substitute with other colors. You can also substitute with other materials. For example, use a small tuft of rabbit fur instead of calftail hair for the head of the fly. The Krystal Flash antennae are not mandatory. And rather than a plastic dumbbell for the eyes, use two pieces of melted monofilament.

The Thing is very lightweight and ideal for casting with lighter tackle. An eight-weight outfit is usually recommended when fishing for bonefish, but when the fish are smaller, or in the evening when the winds drop and you no longer need the casting power of a stouter rod, drop down to a six-weight rod. The smaller rod is a lot of fun to use, especially after casting heavier tackle all day. And catching smaller fish—bonefish, redfish, and more—on the six weight is more enjoyable. Too many anglers think they should always use the same rod, but just like when catching other species of fish, match your tackle to the prevailing conditions.

Goat Belly Shrimp

Hook: Regular saltwater hook, size 4.
Thread: Red 6/0.
Weight: Small chrome dumbbell.
Antennae: Two strands of black Krystal Flash.
Feelers: Black speckled Sili Legs.
Eyes: Melted monofilament.
Egg sac: Orange badger tail fur.
Gills: Natural yellow goat dubbing or Superfine Dubbing.
Wing: Natural badger tail fur.

THE GOAT BELLY SHRIMP IS ANOTHER GREAT S.S. FLIES pattern. This fly contains all the attributes of a first-class shrimp imitation for fishing the flats. Whether you are targeting bonefish, redfish, sea trout, or another species, the Goat Belly Shrimp should be part of your fly selection.

Some tiers go to great lengths to create realistic shrimp imitations, but many of their patterns lack life; they look good in the vise, but seem more static than alive in the water. A better shrimp imitation has a good swimming action; even though the pattern only slightly resembles a shrimp, the materials pulsate when the fly is stripped through the water when retrieved. The fish see this lifelike movement, think it's something good to eat, and strike. If you're casting to a pod of fish, two or three might shift into high gear and burst forward to snatch the fly. Sometimes the action can be quite explosive, especially when casting to marauding redfish. The materials used in the Goat Belly Shrimp flow naturally when retrieving the fly.

A first-rate shrimp imitation should also be heavy enough to drop through the water to the proper depth—from just inches to perhaps two feet—yet not be so heavy that it hits with a loud splash. The fly should land with only a gentle plop. The small chrome dumbbell on the Goat Belly Shrimp is ample to accomplish the task without alarming the fish.

Flying Monkey

Hook: Regular saltwater hook, size 2.
Thread: Tan 3/0.
Head: Deer hair tips.
Eyes: Melted monofilament.
Antennae: Long, thin tan grizzly hackles.
Body: Deer hair.
Weight: Large lead dumbbell.

THIS IS AN UNUSUAL PATTERN, BUT IT HAS A SPECIFIC purpose.

Alan Caolo is a talented fly-pattern designer from Rhode Island. He is also a lecturer, photographer, and author. Alan has written two books that should be in your fly-fishing library. The first is *Fly Fisherman's Guide to Atlantic Baitfish & Other Food Sources*. Read this book if you wish to learn more about what striped bass, bluefish, bonito, and other favorite gamefish are eating. Use this information to create matching imitations.

Alan's other book is titled *Sight-fishing for Striped Bass*. This is a more advanced form of fly fishing. Too many anglers spend their time casting to fish they can't see, hoping their lines go tight with the weight of striking fish. But, much like stalking bonefish and permit flats, you can also stalk and cast to specific striped bass. This requires more hunting and less casting. You're playing the role of predator. And the rewards are more exhilarating.

This pattern, called the Flying Monkey, is the type of fly you will want for sight fishing to striped bass. These fish come onto the flats at high tide in the Northeast. They are looking for small baitfish, sand eels, and especially crabs. The fish will be moving—sometimes at a steady pace—so you will want your fly to drop down the water column quickly. The Flying Monkey has a large dumbbell for weight, but the splash of this pattern rarely spooks the fish; striped bass are not as skittish as bonefish. As the fish approaches, tighten the line and retrieve the fly. The bass will mistake it for a fleeing crab and attack.

Badger Tarpon Fly

Hook: Gamakatsu SC15 or your favorite brand of tarpon hook, size 2/0.
Thread: Chartreuse 3/0.
Eyes: Melted monofilament.
Tail: Chartreuse grizzly hackles.
Collar: Badger fur.

THE BADGER IS A CUSTOM PATTERN OF S.S. FLIES, A LEADING
American-based fly-tying house. These guys work directly with fly shops
and guides to produce the patterns they need to match local fishing conditions. In a world where most shops sell imported flies, often tied in small
factories by workers who have never fly fished, the guys at S.S. Flies are
bona fide fly fishermen.

According to Peter Smith, when describing the unusual collar on this
fly, "Badger fur is wonderful stuff. It has sparse, long black-and-white barred
guard hairs and very fine soft underfur. It's a lot like rabbit fur but twice as
long. Even better is that the underfur shades from a medium gray at the base
to cream at the tips. The Badger Tarpon Fly is tied with the Keys in mind,
but this classic profile and the colors have also been consistently effective
in the Yucatan."

Several furs are suitable for tying the collar on tarpon flies. Coyote is
widely available and inexpensive. Arctic fox tails fur comes in white and
almost any dyed color you could wish. All of these materials are easy to use
and give a fly wonderful swimming action in the water. Rather than using
only hackles for the collars on your tarpon flies, tie a few with hair collars
and see which attracts more fish. I think you will be pleased with the results.

Bunny Shrimp

Hook: Regular saltwater hook, size 2.
Thread: Tan 3/0.
Eyes: Black bead chain.
Tail: Tan Faux Fox with a few strands of pink Krinkle Mirror Flash tied along each side of the tail.
Body: Tan or light brown rabbit underfur clipped from the skin.
Legs: Crazy-Legs, barred and speckled bonefish tan.

THIS FLATS PATTERN IS TIED USING A BLEND OF SYNTHETIC and natural materials. Although this is a slightly large shrimp imitation suitable for permit and redfish, you can easily scale it down in size for targeting bonefish; add a few to your fly box tied in sizes 8 to 4.

The tail of the Bunny Shrimp is tied using a synthetic ingredient called Faux Fox. While I often recommend simple craft fur as a substitute for many synthetic hairs, Faux Fox is not the same type of material. Faux Fox is finer and maintains its bulk on the hook and when fishing; craft fur collapses together when wet, creating a thin streak of collar in the water. Add bars to the tail using a brown permanent marker.

The bead chain, tied to the top of the hook, adds a tad of weight and acts as the eyes on the shrimp. When fishing the flats, the pattern swims in the middle section of the water column.

The body is rabbit underfur. Clip the fur from the hide and pull out the guard hairs. Place the underfur in a dubbing loop with the hairs parallel. Spin the loop closed, and wrap the fur up the hook. Brush back the fur between wraps to prevent binding down any of the fibers. The soft body has terrific swimming action when retrieving the fly.

Swimming Crab

Hook: Long-shank saltwater hook, size 2.
Thread: Tan 3/0.
Weight: A medium lead dumbbell.
Antennae: Tan rabbit fur mixed with Tan UV Krystal Flash.
Eyes: Black plastic beads glued on clear Magic Stretch.
Claws: Puyans Crab Claws.
Shellback: Tan foam topped with Montana Fly Company Crab Skin.
Legs: Tan Sili Legs or rubber legs.
Belly: Tan chamois.

AL RITT'S SWIMMING CRAB IS A NEAT LITTLE PATTERN. A lot of anglers use this type of pattern for catching permit, but it's also a dandy for striped bass. The slap of the fly landing, however, might be a bit much for skittish bonefish cruising skinny-water flats.

The claws are pieces of knotted chenille. They look outstanding!

The eyes are small black plastic beads glued to the ends of pieces of Magic Stretch. The Magic Stretch makes them flexible. You may substitute with monofilament as the eye stalk material, or simply use melted mono-filament eyes. If the melted eyes are not dark enough, paint each eyeball with a drop of black fingernail polish.

The body of this fly is interesting. The top is 1-millimeter-thick foam with a Montana Fly Company Crab Skin glued to the top. You could sub-stitute with Wapsi's Thin Skin, which comes in a wide variety of solid and mottled colors. Be sure to use a flexible, waterproof cement when gluing the top to the foam. Al shapes the body using a cookie-cutter-like tool, but you may use heavy craft scissors. The bottom of the body is a small piece of shaped chamois. Place the rubber legs across the body before gluing together the top and bottom of the fly. The completed body is like a sand-wich with the hook shank running through the middle.

Crab-let

Hook: Regular saltwater hook, size 6.
Thread: Tan 3/0.
Weight: Silver bead chain.
Antennae: Tan rabbit or arctic fox fur mixed with tan UV Krystal Flash.
Body: Tan Cohen's Carp Dub.
Legs: Speckled Sexi Legs.
Belly: Adhesive-backed lead or tungsten tape coated with Clear Cure Goo.

HERE IS ANOTHER AL RITT PATTERN. ALTHOUGH AL LIVES in Colorado, he has a fast-growing reputation for his terrific saltwater patterns. In addition, for the folks who manufacture the Peak Vise, he also leads trips to some of the most desirable fishing destinations in the world.

The Crab-let is a good example of Al's ingenuity at creating flies suitable for catching bonefish, sea trout, and redfish on shallow-water flats. Al weights this fly using only a piece of bead chain. The Crab-let lands gently yet drops through the water column quickly enough to get to the bottom. When the fish approach, tighten your line to raise the fly and make it look like a fleeing crab.

The fur head and rubber legs give the Crab-let a soft, flowing action in the water. You may substitute with narrow-diameter rubber legs for the Sexi Legs.

Cohen's Carp Dub is a new product. Pat Cohen is a leading pattern designer who is setting the fly-tying world on fire. He had an idea for a new type of dubbing. Rather than spending "hours with an old coffee grinder in hand and various bags of materials," Pat teamed up with the folks at Hareline Dubbin to create this new dubbing. Although originally designed for tying carp patterns, Al Ritt quickly adapted this all-synthetic material to his saltwater flies. The completed body looks outstanding. (Of course, you may substitute with your favorite brand of synthetic dubbing.)

For additional weight, Al places a small piece of adhesive-backed lead or tungsten tape under the body. He coats the tape with Clear Cure Goo or another light-cured adhesive, and then trims the body to shape.

Bird Fur Shrimp

Hook: Regular saltwater hook, size 2.
Thread: Pink 3/0.
Weight: Gold bead chain.
Eyes: Black plastic beads on clear stems.
Antennae: Bonefish pink Loco Legs.
Body: Pink midge Diamond Braid.
Hackle: Pink Whiting Farms Bird Fur.

THE BIRD FUR SHRIMP IS AN INTERESTING PATTERN design. Lightweight and wispy, this pattern suggests life when swimming through the water. The Bird Fur Shrimp lands gently so it will not spook fish when wading even heavily pressured flats. This is also another pattern that you can use with lighter weight tackle in the evening when the winds drop or when casting to smaller fish.

Bird Fur is a product of Whiting Farms. Whiting Farms is the leader in producing what is called "genetic" dry fly hackle. In addition to these marvelous hackles, Whiting Farms produces a wide variety of other fly-tying feathers. Bird Fur is one example.

Bird Fur was originally designed as a substitute for heron feathers when tying Atlantic salmon and steelhead Spey flies. These fibers are extremely long and give a fly a lot of life in the water. The problem is that it is illegal to use real heron feathers. Bird Fur is a fine substitute.

According to Whiting Farms, they spent nine years developing this unique product. Although it looks like fur on the skin, these are long, fine-fibered feathers. These feathers come from the saddle areas of roosters. A package of Bird Fur contains one-half of the saddle, enough feathers for tying dozens and dozens of flies.

Although originally designed for making salmon and Spey flies, you can also use Bird Fur when tying original saltwater patterns.

Spawning Ghost

Hook: Regular saltwater hook, size 2.
Thread: Tan 3/0.
Eyes: Gold bead chain.
Tail: Tan UV Krystal Flash.
Antennae: Perfectly barred Sili Legs.
Egg sac: Orange McFly Foam.
Body: Opal Mirage Flash.
Body veil: Amber Antron yarn.
Wing: Perfectly barred Sili Legs.

IT'S SURPRISING HOW MANY IMITATIONS OF SPAWNING shrimp have been created. There are dozens of flies purporting to match shrimp carrying orange egg sacs. A lot of experienced anglers swear that these patterns catch more fish than flies without egg sacs. Why is this?

The fish, of course, are not distinguishing between shrimp—and shrimp imitations—that do have egg sacs and those that do not. One type of shrimp isn't better than the other. Instead, the brightly colored egg sac makes the fly stand out in the water and acts as a target for feeding fish.

In the world of freshwater nymph fishing, flies with "hot spots" and brightly colored beads have become all the rage. Anglers insist that these patterns catch more trout. I have experimented with these patterns, and I also believe they catch more fish. The same is true of a spawning shrimp imitation. The bright orange egg sac acts like a hot spot so the fish can more easily see the fly.

Al Ritt made the egg sac on this Spawning Ghost using orange McFly Foam, but you may substitute with Antron yarn or even chenille. If your local fly shop doesn't stock barred Sili Legs, select another brand of speckled rubber legs.

Note the veil of Antron yarn over the top of the body. This feature gives the fly a slightly transparent appearance similar to a real shrimp. The overall tan color matches a real shrimp; shrimp turn orange, a common fly-tying color, only after cooking.

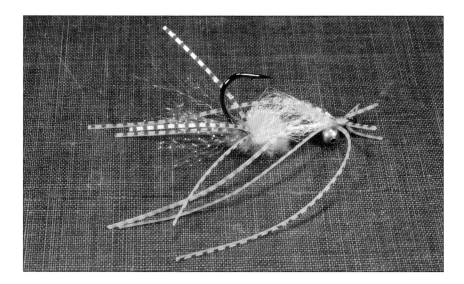

Foxy Shrimp

Hook: Regular saltwater hook, size 2.
Thread: Orange 3/0.
Eyes: Pink bead chain.
Egg sac: Orange Sparkle Yarn.
Antennae: Black Krystal Flash.
Tail: Tan arctic fox fur.
Eyes: Black glass beads mounted on Stretch Magic.
Head: Shrimp pink UV Ice Dub.
Legs: Perfectly barred Sili Legs.
Body: Shrimp pink UV Ice Dub.
Wing: Tan arctic fox fur.
Topping: Pink Krinkle Mirror Flash.

I HAVE ALWAYS TAUGHT MY FLY-TYING STUDENTS THAT one of the attributes of a good tier is that all of his flies look somewhat alike. Even when the exact patterns change, they look as though they were made by the same tier. The tier has a style. He might make bulky or sparse flies. He might have a preference for using synthetic or natural ingredients. He might emphasize the outline of the bait he is imitating, or he might put more emphasis on movement.

A novice's flies are all over the place, even when tying the exact same pattern: some are sparse, some are bulky, some are small, and some are large. A new tier often pays little attention to detail, and it shows in his collection of flies. Develop a sense for style and proportions, and your flies will immediately become more professional looking.

The Foxy Shrimp is another Al Ritt pattern. And, like all of his other shrimp imitations, it is very sparse and emphasizes movement. The more I look at his flies, the easier it has become to pick them out of a crowded fly box. They have a style all their own, and they do catch fish.

A new tier would do well and catch more fish if they studied Al's tying style and also made sparse patterns that emphasized lifelike action and movement.

Quivering Fringe

Hook: Regular saltwater hook, size 1.
Thread: Yellow 3/0.
Weight: Medium gold dumbbell.
Egg sac: Orange wool.
Claws: Olive hackles.
Feelers: Orange speckled Sili Legs.
Eyes: Melted monofilament.
Head and body: Olive-brown Chick-a-bou.
Back: Olive EP Fibers.

S.S. FLIES CREATED THE QUIVERING FRINGE FOR CAPTAIN Will Benson. In fact, Captain Benson was the first professional guide to work with S.S. Flies—even before it was called S.S. Flies. He wanted custom patterns to match his local fishing conditions in Key West.

The Quivering Fringe was originally conceived as a permit pattern. The heavy dumbbell makes the fly drop quickly through the water column to the proper depth. When resting on the sand bottom, the rubber legs, positioned on the bottom of the fly, keep the claws cocked upright.

Chick-a-bou is another product of Whiting Farms. These feathers come from the belly of a chicken between the legs. Chick-a-bou is used as a substitute for small marabou feathers. The fibers are extremely soft and give a fly a lot of life in the water. You can purchase small patches of Chick-a-bou, or an entire Chick-a-bou skin, at your local fly shop. Chick-a-bou comes in a wide range of natural and dyed colors, so there is something to make almost any fly you wish.

The Quivering Fringe is a stylized crab imitation. Fish it with slow strips to imitate a fleeing crab. Although it was designed to catch permit, it has proven itself on the bonefish flats. It is also a terrific choice when casting to redfish, sea trout, and other species of gamefish that feed on crabs.